WAVES AND PLAGUES

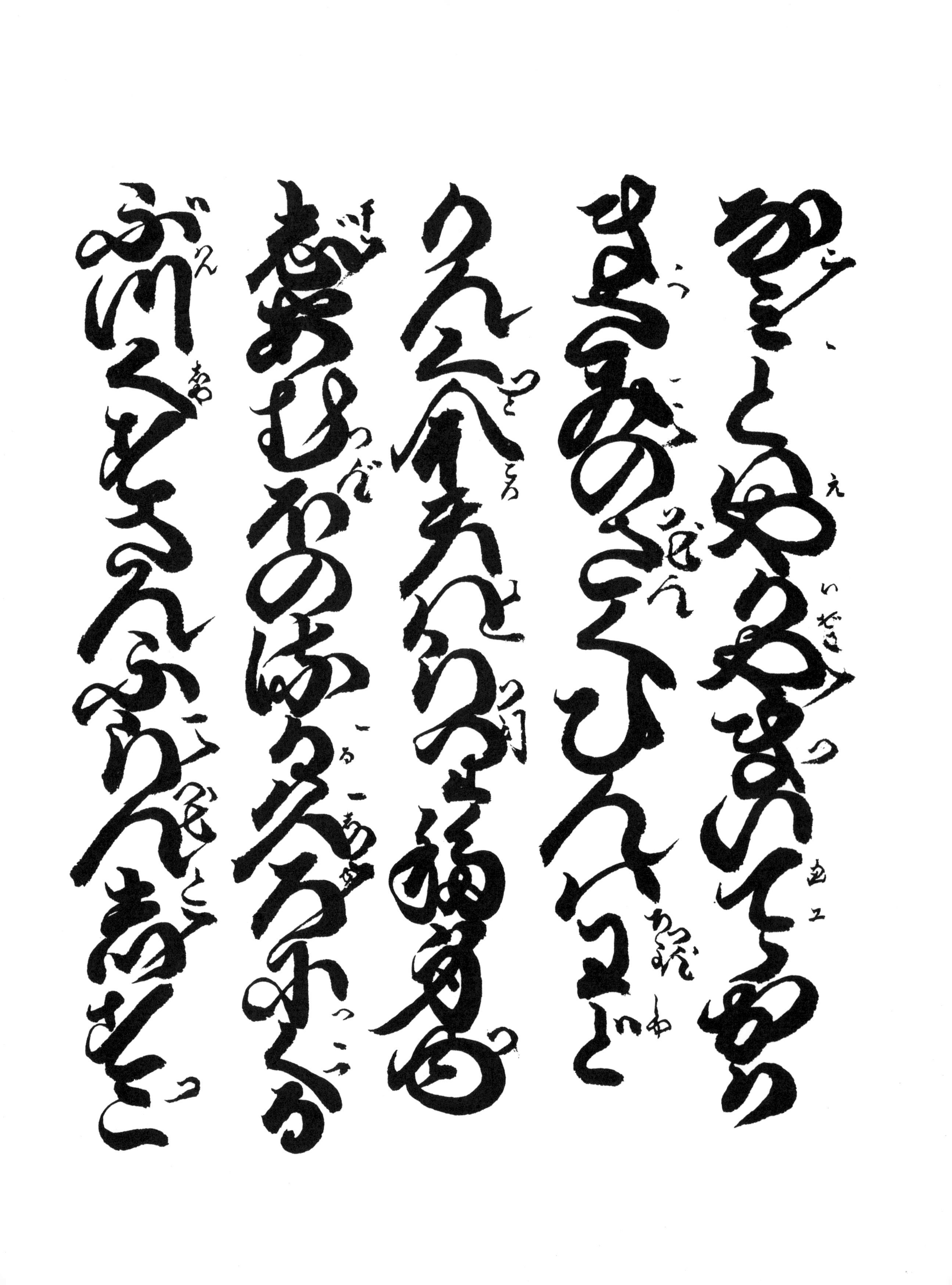

[illegible]

[illegible]

[illegible]

[illegible]

[illegible]

WAVES AND PLAGUES

THE ART OF

MASAMI TERAOKA

BY HOWARD A. LINK

THE CONTEMPORARY MUSEUM
HONOLULU

CHRONICLE BOOKS
SAN FRANCISCO

This book has been made possible, in part, by a grant from the National Endowment for the Arts.

Exhibition Schedule

The Contemporary Museum, Honolulu
October 22, 1988–February 13, 1989

Long Beach Museum of Art, Long Beach, California
March 19–April 23, 1989

Photo Credits: Susan Einstein, pp. 11, 55; Marva Marrow, p. 8.
Photography of the artist's work by Lynda Hess and Masami Teraoka.
Note: Cat. no. 18 will not be shown in Honolulu.

Produced by Ed Marquand Book Design

Cover: *AIDS Series/Geisha in Bath,* 1988 (cat. no. 25).
Back cover: *AIDS Series/Black Ships and Geisha*, 1987 (cat. no. 27).

Library of Congress Cataloging-in-Publication Data

Link, Howard A.
Waves and plagues.

"The Contemporary Museum, Honolulu."
Bibliography: p.
1. Teraoka, Masami, 1936– —Themes, motives—Exhibitions. I. Contemporary Museum (Honolulu, Hawaii) II. Title.
NS1839.T47A4 1988 759.13 88-25773
ISBN 0-87701-602-X
ISBN 0-87701-590-2 (pbk.)

Printed in Japan

Chronicle Books
275 Fifth Street
San Francisco, California 94103

CONTENTS

ACKNOWLEDGMENTS

It is with great pleasure that The Contemporary Museum, as its premier exhibition, presents new works by one of America's modern masters, Masami Teraoka. I wish to extend my gratitude to the museum's Board of Trustees, for believing in and supporting this project from the very beginning, and to several individuals without whose able assistance the exhibition and book would not have been possible.

First, my appreciation goes to Masami Teraoka for exploring new levels of creativity and for his tireless, always cheerful assistance with all aspects of the exhibition and catalogue's development. Lynda Hess successfully shouldered the multiple responsibilities of archivist, photographer, and liaison for Masami and essayist Howard Link. Roger Keyes has written an insightful foreword, and Edward Den Lau, of Space Gallery, Los Angeles, helped to secure loans of important recent paintings now in the hands of collectors. My thanks to each of the lenders to the exhibition for generously allowing us temporary possession of their prized works.

The real hero of this undertaking is Dr. Howard Link. His recent transition to the post of senior curator emeritus of Asian art at the Honolulu Academy of Arts enabled him to devote his precious time to this project. No one is better suited to explain and interpret Teraoka's particular blend of East and West than Dr. Link, who has known and written about Teraoka for many years. My sincere gratitude goes to him for his scholarship in producing this fine text.

Others deserving special recognition are Marion Campbell, for typing these many, many pages; Suzanne Kotz, for her superior editing; and Ed Marquand, for the swift, sure organization and design of this handsome book.

And, of course, kudos to "the staff of many hats" at The Contemporary Museum: Loraine Pang, Catherine Wheeler, Deborah Dunn, Chrys Cundiff, Jessica Putnam, and Brenda Santos. They attended to all the crushing details of organizing a major exhibition and catalogue while at the same time preparing to open the doors of the new museum.

We who live here at the geographical center of the Pacific Rim are privileged to share Hawaii with Masami Teraoka and to provide the launching pad for his wit and wisdom-filled art missiles aimed in both directions, East and West.

FRITZ A. FRAUCHIGER
Director, The Contemporary Museum
Honolulu

FOREWORD

Masami Teraoka is a genius. I do not want to frighten you; his paintings are not esoteric, they are brilliant. They are serious, but never ponderous. They combine qualities we do not expect to find in the same picture: they can be sensual and comic, wild and sharp, grave and ironic.

Teraoka learned to combine these qualities from two teachers, Utagawa Kunisada (1786–1864) and Katsushika Hokusai (1760–1849). These great Japanese artists also taught him how to draw. More precisely, Teraoka formed his unmistakably personal style of drawing figures and landscape by studying Hokusai's brush paintings and Kunisada's color prints. But the word "study" hardly suggests the tremendously disciplined effort of a classical artist like Teraoka.

The classical quest to penetrate the mind of your teachers and rekindle their spirit in your own work requires a temporary but complete surrender and fastidious, constant effort. Teraoka has made this commitment. The groundbreaking new paintings in this volume show us the fusion between East and West, past and present, personal and universal, that can result when commitment is supported by intelligence, sensibility, and talent.

There are two kinds of paintings: those the artist can change and those the artist cannot. Teraoka paints in black ink and water-based colors on paper, an unforgiving medium. Every line has to be right the first time. There are no second chances. Once he begins his final drawing, he cannot hesitate. He is completely exposed, with no place to hide. Teraoka puts himself at risk every time he paints, and perhaps that is one reason his recent AIDS paintings are so poignant. In several of these paintings he has left some of his tentative, sketchy underdrawing, and we can actually see what risks he takes.

A hero conquers fear by facing danger. It takes courage to do this. Teraoka has found a model for courage in the few surviving paintings by a third teacher, the legendary Japanese swordsman, Miyamoto Musashi (1584–1645). In Teraoka's new landscapes we see some of the qualities born of courage: strength, clarity, and stillness. Masami Teraoka is more than a genius; he is a hero. His work is an inspiration.

ROGER KEYES
Director, Center for the Study of
Japanese Woodblock Prints
Woodacre, California

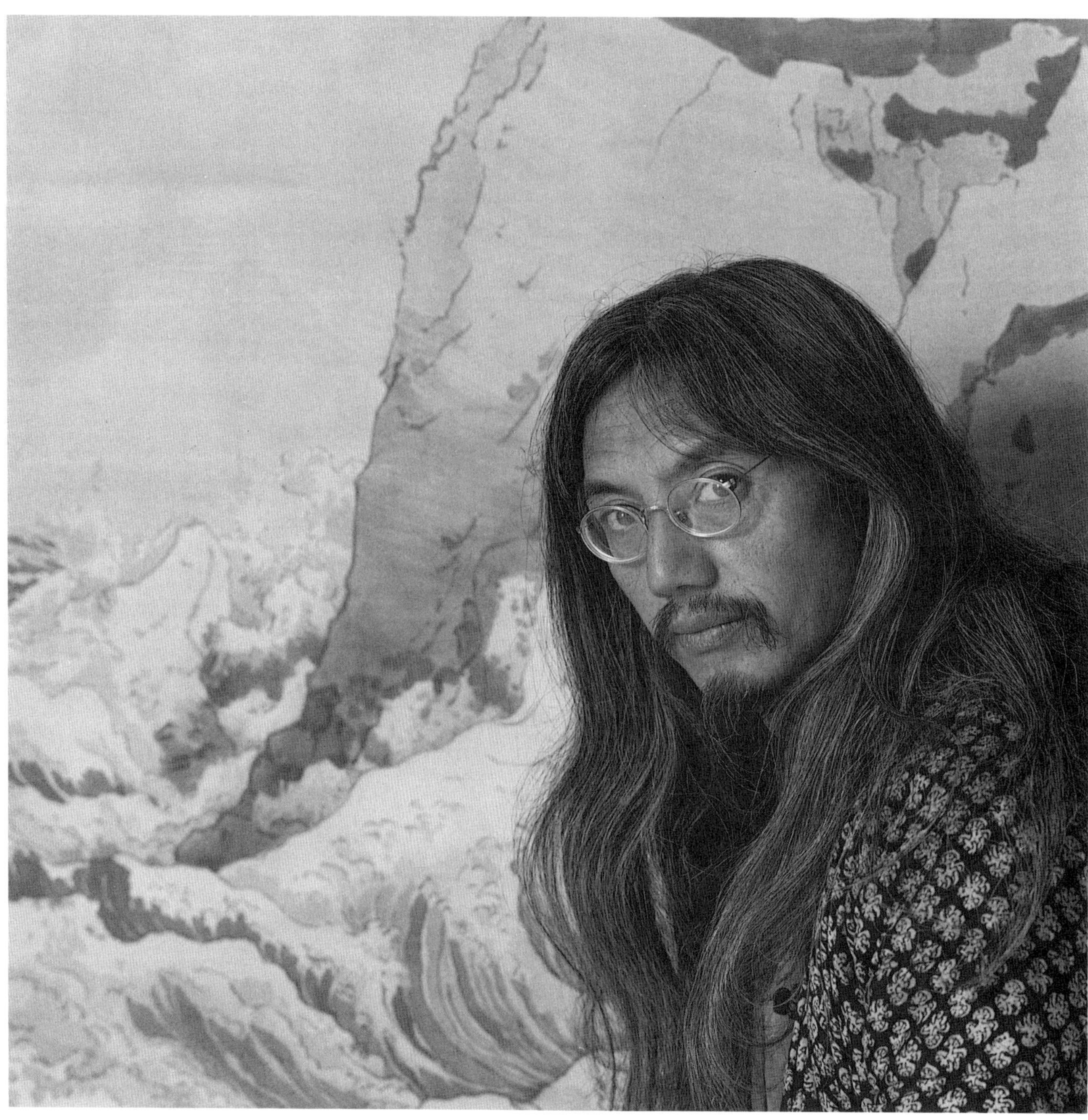

Fig. 1. Masami Teraoka.

PREFACE

We were making the long trip from Honolulu by way of the Koolau mountain range and the superb Pali Lookout to the east shore studio of Masami Teraoka. Fritz Frauchiger, director of Honolulu's Contemporary Museum, was driving. Ahead of us was a busload of Japanese tourists, and during a lull in our conversation, my mind imagined how Teraoka might render the scene. He would no doubt draw upon the meticulously controlled style of nineteenth-century Japanese woodblocks, as he has done for the last several years, treating the event with humor and insight. He would bring the same superb technique and keen perceptions to this scene as he does to the hypocrisies that obsess our world. I imagined Masami's vision: a vigorous procession of timeless figures headed by four men hurrying back and forth and shouting, "Bow down! Bow down!" Two stout servants follow, bearing tall staffs heavily plumed on top; behind them stride a number of unusual warriors. Bare-kneed, they wear leggings and loose sandals. Over plain gray garments are colorful coats, from which protrude two carefully arranged golf clubs, Teraoka's symbol of the corporate samurai. The clubs have been thrust, as if they were swords, into the heavy belts that encircle the samurais' waists. Each man wears a big circular straw hat, which remains steady as he marches, golf clubs jut out fore and aft, and shoulders move in an exaggerated manner. The crests of Toshiba, Sony, Mitsubishi, and a host of other great corporate-warrior families can be recognized among the array of floating banners. The faces of the warriors are solemn and preoccupied, for they are samurai, "those who serve." Behind these stocky men come nearly a hundred others, some lugging huge boxes full of photographic equipment, some carrying portable TV cameras, still others munching on hamburgers and french fries. Each item of cargo is stamped with the bright crest of the Japan Travel Bureau, and several solemn men (daimyo presidents) ride hunched up, knees to the chin, smoking cigarettes, in a miniature bus. Behind come dozens of servants, some with tall poles tipped with banners, others leading horses, some carrying boxes filled with sushi. One servant carries aloft a warning plume, and two handymen scurry about crying a last warning, "Bow down!" At the close of this bizarre scene, two Westerners in a small American-made automobile sputter along, attempting to keep up with the curious cavalcade; the past and the present, the East and the West meet. "I've missed the turnoff, Howard." With these words, my mind returned to the real sojourn, and as Fritz turned back a block, I realized we had made much of the trip to Teraoka's studio in silence.

Despite the fact that Teraoka had moved to Hawaii in 1980, this was my first visit to his studio on the east shore of Oahu, and I was curious as to what I would find. Teraoka, who was born and raised in Japan, has lived in the United States for more than two decades and, for the last eight years, has divided his time between Hawaii and the mainland. He is now regarded as the best chronicler of some of the many changes brought about by the association and exchange between the United States and Japan. Yet as an artist, Teraoka is no mere recorder of the scene, but a commentator and a social critic who reacts to and comments on contemporary society. He has illuminated many of the worst aspects of Japanese and American culture in works abundantly rich both in appearance and narrative content.

"Irasshai!" Masami stood at the gate to welcome us to his home. Dressed in a summer *yukata* and sandals, with his long salt-and-pepper hair and disheveled beard (fig. 1), he reminded me of a Buddhist pilgrim or a mountain priest *(yamabushi)*. "Hisashiburi, Hawado-san." "Yes, it's been much too long," I replied.

The studio, a typical Hawaiian dwelling of modest size, contained an odd assortment of Eastern and Western paraphernalia. The hardwood floors were lightly stained and buffed to a high finish. The rooms were painted white; no pictures graced their walls. Covering a piano was a huge gray cloth with a family crest *(mon)* reversed in white. As Masami ushered us out into the backyard, my mind once again wandered. I have always pictured Masami as an incarnation of the eccentric ukiyo-e masters of old. As a modern-day Hokusai, how might he reveal his latest work to us? Perhaps he would have lined off part of the yard with a huge wind curtain (*maku*). On the ground would be a massive canvas, as big, perhaps, as an average Japanese room. Roped to pulleys, the painting could be hauled aloft for viewing when completed. Teraoka would go to work, surrounded by vats of lampblack and color and Japanese brushes of all sizes, his antique spectacles askew. He would kneel, tucking his feet neatly under him, as he meditated on how to begin (fig. 2). Then slowly he would trace the portrait of a beautiful woman, a bust portrait *(ōkubi-e)* in the manner of Utagawa Kunisada (1786–1864) or Utagawa Kuniyoshi (1797–1861), his ukiyo-e idols. Finally, Teraoka would pause and ask us to pull on the ropes to bring the painting into position. The vast expanse of canvas would rise into the air and disclose Masami's miracle.

At this point I became earthbound again, and found myself viewing a picture more powerful than my fantasy—the outlines of a beautiful lady (cat. no. 25). The artist had painted a portrait so large that it overwhelmed the eye; yet, after weeks of laborious detailing, the monumental work would be so minutely refined that a magnifying glass would be needed to take it all in.

It seems appropriate that in forming his style Teraoka turned to the art of nineteenth-century Japanese ukiyo-e printmakers, who used a special kind of overripe beauty as a vehicle for hidden messages of wit and satire. Ukiyo means "the floating world," and in the Edo period (1615–1868) the term connoted a predilection for the pleasures of the transitory, everyday

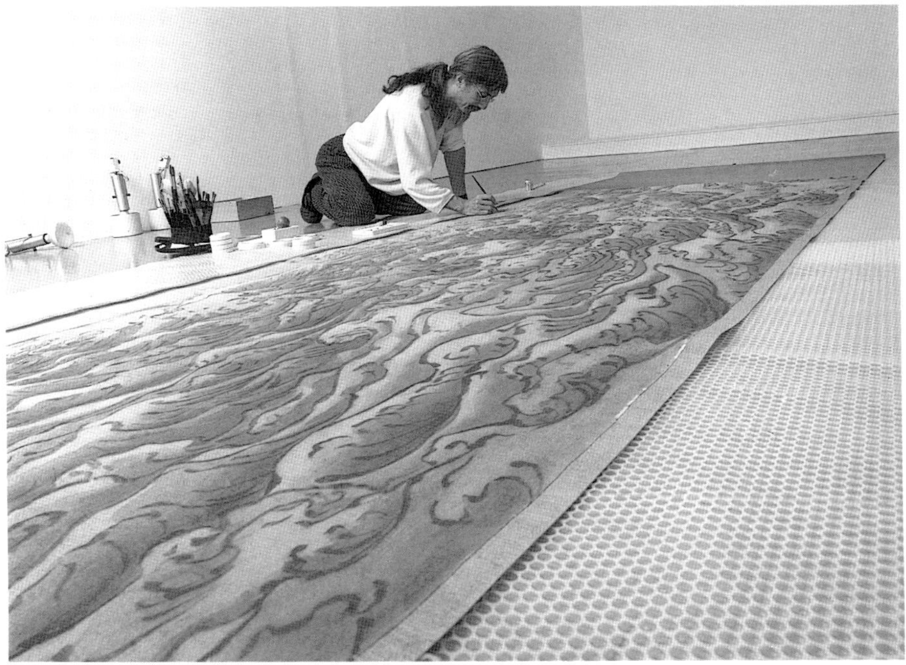

Fig. 2. Masami Teraoka at work.

world. The term also came to describe the genre pictures that depicted this world, most notably woodblock prints, or ukiyo-e, which covered a wide range of popular subjects, kabuki plays, portraits of actors and courtesans, landscape views, and erotica. In their delicate color gradations and the inclusion of seals, calligraphy, and elaborately framed cartouches, Teraoka's works mimic nineteenth-century Japanese woodblock prints. But Teraoka's medium is watercolor, and his elongated formats are more like handscrolls than the small rectangular shapes of ukiyo-e prints. Like ukiyo-e artists, Teraoka delights in blending nuances of hidden meaning, often erotic or salacious, but sometimes serious and poignant. Keen wit, twists of earthy humor, and visual and verbal puns are combined with sumptuous colors and patterns in a sophisticated style that is deceptively complex in meaning. Although the casual viewer can appreciate the rich designs and technical virtuosity in the works, a full understanding of many of them can only be achieved through knowledge of the subject and careful reading of the seals and inscriptions.

Teraoka has said of his work, "The message and the beauty go hand in hand. The balance of the two is of the utmost importance." His meticulously finished paintings are extraordinarily beautiful, but their detailed elegance does not dilute or soften their content; rather, it attracts and involves the eye while the mind becomes aware of the subtle wit, humor, parody, and satire to be found in them. Aesthetic form and sophisticated content sharpen one another in an ingenious mixture unique to Masami Teraoka.

As dusk settled in, Masami reviewed and explained all that we had seen: thirty-three major paintings of incredible skill—fluid creations that sometimes point out the absurdities of man's dilemma and at other times reflect the majesty and mystery of nature. Still other works address questions of humanity's future on this planet. These paintings take on a more serious mood—the art of a man humble enough to understand his own mortality.

WAVES AND PLAGUES: THE ART OF MASAMI TERAOKA

THE MAN AND HIS ART

Masami Teraoka arrived at his unique blend of traditional Japanese form and contemporary attitudes through rigorous training. Born in Onomichi, Japan, in 1936, he first studied watercolor painting under a local artist, Moemon Sugihara (act. 1930s–1940s). Teraoka's interest in ukiyo-e woodblock prints came as the result of exposure to a small collection of nineteenth-century prints owned by his grandparents. At the time he never suspected that these "magnificent scraps of paper" would become the source of inspiration for his own painting. That would come much later.

Onomichi, then a town of about 130,000 inhabitants, is a harbor community located in the eastern part of Hiroshima prefecture, not far from Okayama prefecture and the Inland Sea. It is a beautiful place, and one can travel in a matter of minutes from the sea to the mountains; in this respect it is not unlike Hawaii, Teraoka's present home, although the vegetation is very different because of a cooler climate. Teraoka recalls that the beaches were not as beautiful as those in Hawaii, and the waves were not as large or as rough. It was the Onomichi landscape that young Teraoka often painted under the guidance of his teacher.

Masami's parents realized that their son possessed a special talent, and they both encouraged him to pursue an artistic career. His father particularly enjoyed Western-style singing, and his mother appreciated art and could draw with skill. In fact, a cousin on his mother's side, Chikkyō Ono (b. 1889), achieved great fame as a traditional painter in the Taishō period (1912–26). Chikkyō's landscape paintings combined Western and Japanese styles and, although very different from the ukiyo-e/pop style that Masami prefers, show the same Japanese preference for flat color forms and a distinctive allocation of space. In this there is a fundamental relationship between the two artists' approaches. Teraoka owns an album of landscapes by Chikkyo Ono's brother, Chikutō, and sometimes refers to it for inspiration, particularly when painting a pure landscape (fig. 3).

Moemon Sugihara was not as great an artist as Chikkyō Ono or Chikutō Ono, but he was a particularly gifted teacher. After two years with Sugihara, Teraoka continued to study watercolor independently, perfecting his skills and learning to control his brush to create a precise but fluid line, layering tints and applying even washes free from the accidental pools of color that characterize most watercolor techniques today. In these early years Teraoka helped in his family's kimono shop, where he encountered firsthand many striking patterns that would later serve as an important source for his detailed ukiyo-e style art. Indeed, Teraoka often introduces the family crest of that kimono store into his art in the form of a publisher's seal.

During the Second World War the Teraoka family was forced to go without most luxuries. Masami owned no toys and, although he had three sisters, generally preferred to be alone. His painting was the central focus of his life, and his parents provided him with whatever art supplies they could afford. When Teraoka was nine years old, his father brought him a thick full-color book of Western-style paintings by Japanese artists, and impressed by their work, he wished to study and learn from them.

Because of Masami's obvious gift, his father wanted him to pursue painting studies at the Tokyo Fine Arts Institute rather then attend a formal university. But Masami rebelled and insisted on attending Kwansei Gakuin University in Kobe. There he majored in aesthetics, which introduced him to many facets of art, drama, and literature—a broad range of creative subjects that would serve him well in the years to come. During five years of study at the university, Teraoka continued to paint. Bright, flat color areas and the abstract allocation of space already interested him and were entering his artistic vocabulary. He became fascinated with the architectonic style and juxtaposition of colors found in the art of Piet Mondrian (1872–1944) and produced paintings in a technique that combined Mondrian's style with something of Josef Albers (1888–1976). That he should be attracted to the art of Mondrian is understandable, since the Japanese use of architectural space in elements such as shoji screens offers a similar aesthetic.

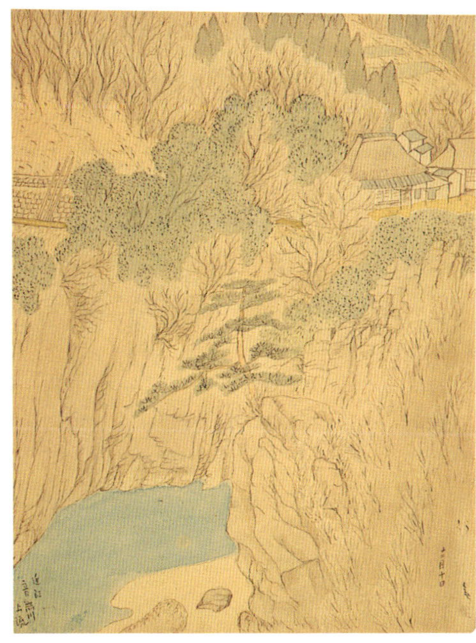

Fig. 3. Chikutō Ono, *Landscape*, Taishō period, watercolor, 11 1/2 × 8 1/2 inches, collection of Masami Teraoka.

In 1961, after graduation and at the suggestion of his father, Teraoka moved to America to study art in earnest. He recalls:

> It was very exciting and yet very terrible. My English was so poor that I couldn't communicate. I only had a one-way ticket and $600 in my pocket. That wouldn't take me very far. First, I studied at the Los Angeles Harbor College for two years. It was my teacher at Harbor College, Harold Jones, who suggested that I concentrate on fine art as opposed to the applied arts. He recommended the Otis Art Institute, and it was at this fine art school that I began to think in terms of a fine arts career.

During this restless period Teraoka witnessed the emergence of pop art. His work was influenced by the eccentric subject matter of this movement, particularly by the flat, solid color shapes of Tom Wesselmann. In 1971 Teraoka began combining elements of ukiyo-e prints with pop art in a series

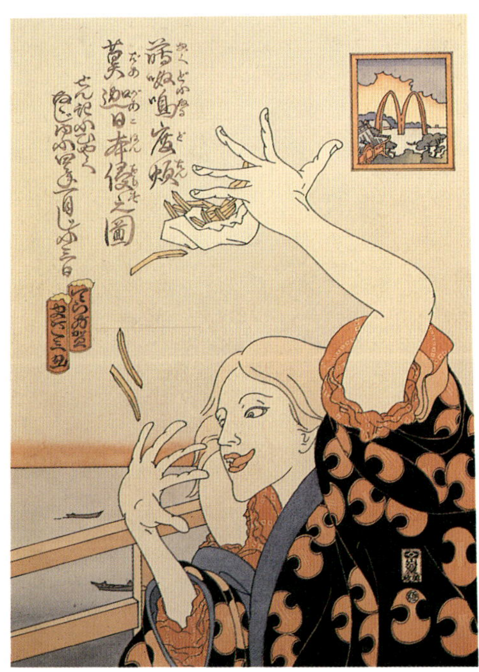

Fig. 4. *McDonald's Hamburgers Invading Japan/ Flying Fries*, 1974, watercolor on paper, 20 × 14 inches, collection of Dr. Ray Mnich, Beverly Hills, California.

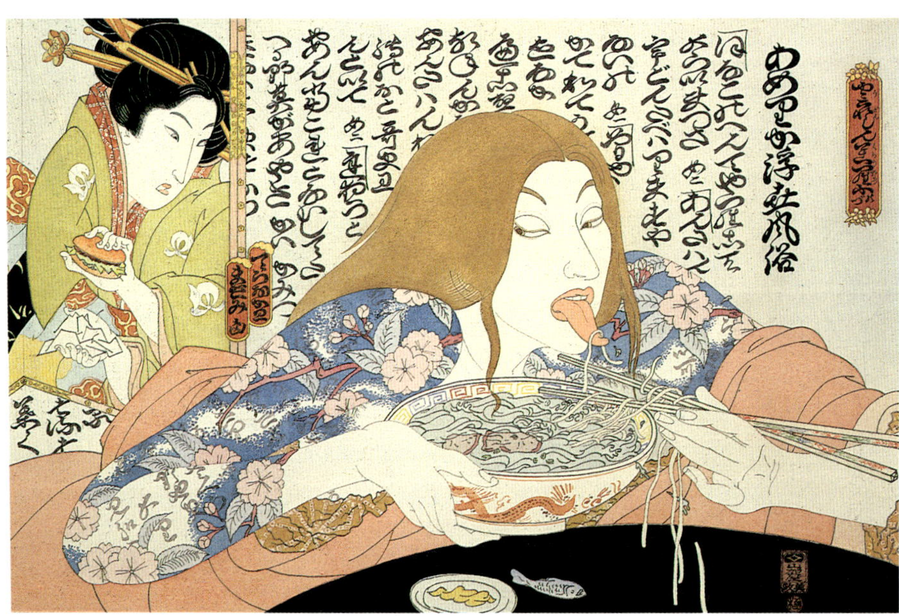

Fig. 5. *McDonald's Hamburgers Invading Japan/Geisha and Tattooed Woman*, 1975, watercolor on paper, 14 1/4 × 21 1/2 inches, collection of Mr. and Mrs. Richard Danziger, New York.

done in various media, *Hollywood Landscape*. In the same year he also produced his first important watercolors, an erotic set aptly entitled *Ukiyo-e Series*. In these works Teraoka introduced the attenuated figures of nude Caucasian women with curious facial features and long manes of hair. They appear in one passionate episode after another, often in ungainly configurations, and sometimes dressed in traditional kimonos. Sexual imagery and innuendo abound. Teraoka's frank visualization of human beings caught up in obsessive sex is of particular significance to an understanding of his later work of the 1970s, for in it much of this early eroticism was subtly retained. He would return again to erotica in the 1980s, in his remarkable *Wave* series (cat. nos. 6–9).

The late 1960s and the early 1970s represent the turning point in Masami's development, for he then hit upon the idea of combining traditional Japanese symbolism, as represented in the numerous facets of ukiyo-e (parody, erotica, kabuki, etc.), with his knowledge of American culture, gained by a decade of life in the U.S. and by observation of its pop art movement. Pop art and ukiyo-e, able to communicate a message via their content, provided not only a vehicle by which Teraoka could express his philosophy of and growing concern with the human condition, but a medium for his considerable humor.

In 1974 Teraoka began a major series of paintings in the ukiyo-e style entitled *McDonald's Hamburgers Invading Japan*. This series pokes fun at American fast food and the eagerness of the Japanese to adopt Western ways. The first painting in the series, *Flying Fries* (fig. 4), shows the long-haired female type of Teraoka's earlier erotic pictures dressed in a kimono, a bag of McDonald's french fries flying out of her hand. The humorous characterization of this awkward creature, wildly attempting to eat the fries, her tongue hanging out, implies that a culture that has trouble holding greasy fries is definitely on a collision course with Americanization.

Another work from the series, *Geisha and Tattooed Woman* (fig. 5), developed the theme still further. The central figure, her shoulders and arms completely covered with tattooed kimono-like patterns and calligraphic verse, tackles a bowl of Japanese soup noodles. Her tongue provocatively twists around the noodles with slippery delight. Depicted in the same Westernized style as the woman in *Flying Fries*, she is in sharp contrast to the jutting-jawed courtesan in the background, borrowed from the work of a nineteenth-century ukiyo-e artist, Utagawa Kunisada (1786–1864), who would become Teraoka's idol. Peeping around a sliding door like a voyeur in a classic erotic scene, the courtesan clutches a hamburger in one hand and in the other a rumpled napkin, a modern version of a favorite nineteenth-century Japanese erotic convention. The long inscription, written in the style reserved for Japanese erotic pictures, is a suggestive dialogue about the proper way to eat Japanese food. The tattooed woman opens, "Well, I'm going to start eating now." She is countered with a query from the envious courtesan: "Are you really going to eat that Japanese noodle soup?" The tattooed woman replies, "Yes, I'm starved. I hope you don't mind my slurping." The courtesan, unable to contain herself any longer, demands, "How am I supposed to eat this? Should I just bite into it?"

The stumpy, hunched-up women of Kunisada's prints from the Tempō era (c. 1830s) often serve as models for Teraoka. Although ungraceful to the modern eye, the unhealthy postures depicted by these portraits were typical of the day: constrictive clothing and years of sitting hunched over on tatami and cushions led to a bearing much in keeping with the Utagawa style of the nineteenth century. The foreshortened trunk, the thick short neck, and the knock knees that Utagawa Toyokuni (1769–1825) created for his *bijin* (beautiful women), a style perpetuated by his followers, were closely associated with the practical details of life in Edo at the time and would in no sense have seemed unnatural to his contemporaries. That Teraoka should choose this fulsome style to depict his ukiyo-e fantasies is quite purposeful. Not only is Utagawa Kunisada (Toyokuni's student) one of Teraoka's ukiyo-e heroes, but his overripe style suits the "overripe" conditions of Japan today.

Other works from the series convey a quieter, more delicate, even decorative mood. In *Tokyo Ginza Shuffle* (fig. 6), Teraoka's mastery of line and spatial relationships and composition is demonstrated in a glimpse of the sandal-clad feet of strolling women and the hems of their beautifully patterned kimonos. A hamburger, surprisingly intact, and a couple of fries and napkins lying on the ground are the only indications that this elegant painting is part of the *McDonald's Hamburgers Invading Japan* series. These

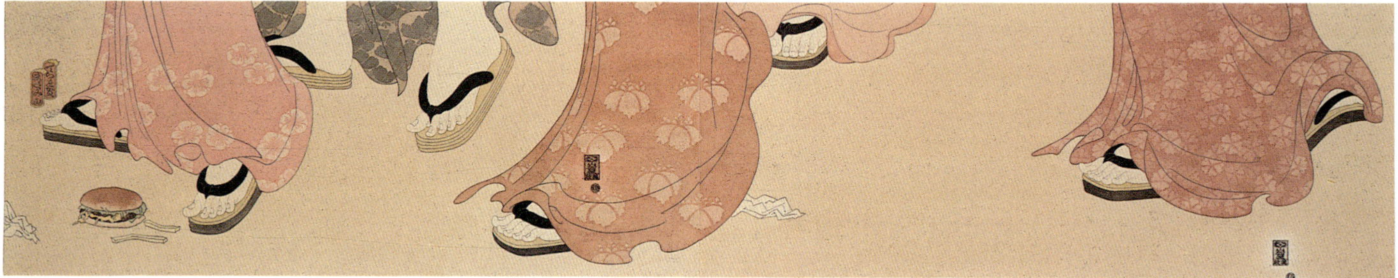

Fig. 6. *McDonald's Hamburgers Invading Japan/Tokyo Ginza Shuffle*, 1974, watercolor on paper, 11 × 55 inches, collection of Esther Richmond, Los Angeles.

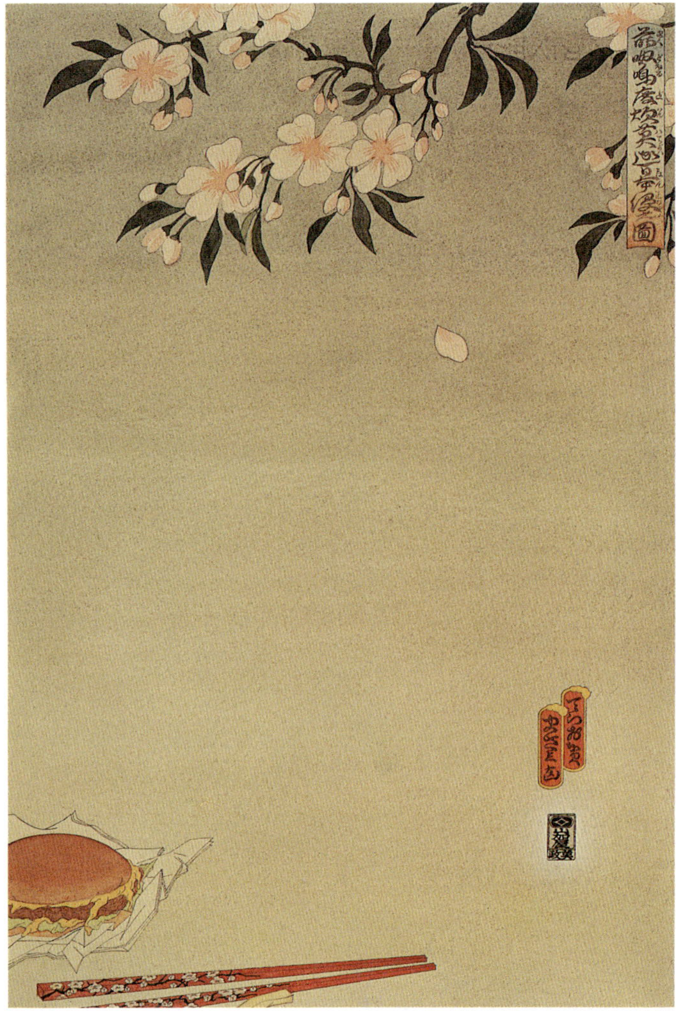

Fig. 7. *McDonald's Hamburgers Invading Japan/Hamburger and Chopsticks*, 1976, watercolor on paper, 21 1/2 × 14 1/2 inches. Frederick R. Weisman Collection.

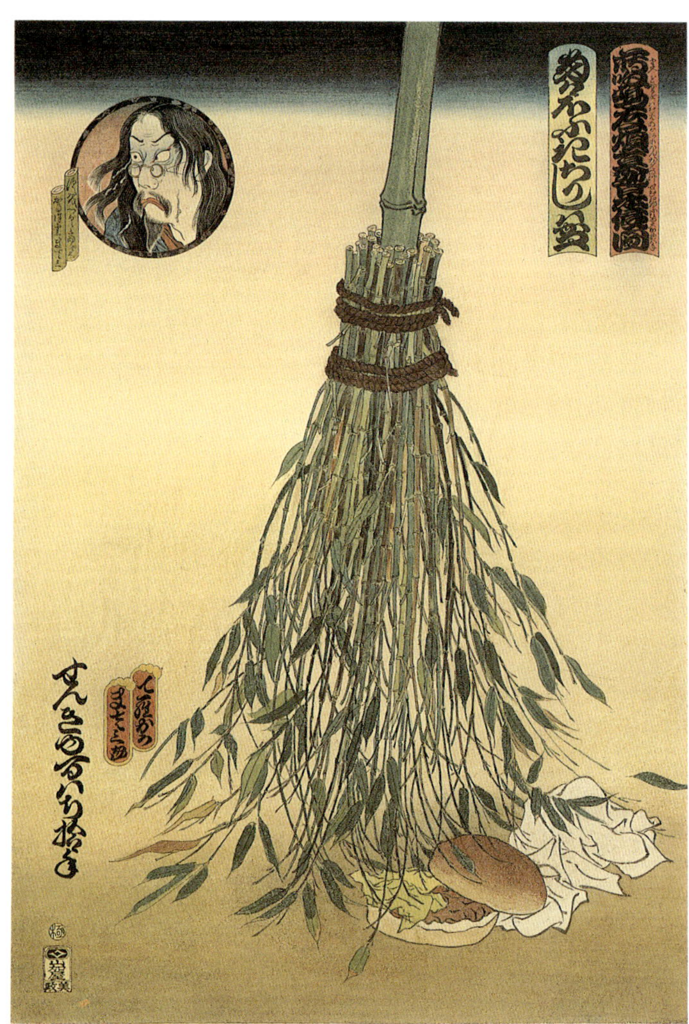

Fig. 8. *McDonald's Hamburgers Invading Japan/Self-Portrait*, 1980, watercolor on paper, 24 1/2 × 17 inches, collection of Helen Sheets, Santa Monica, California.

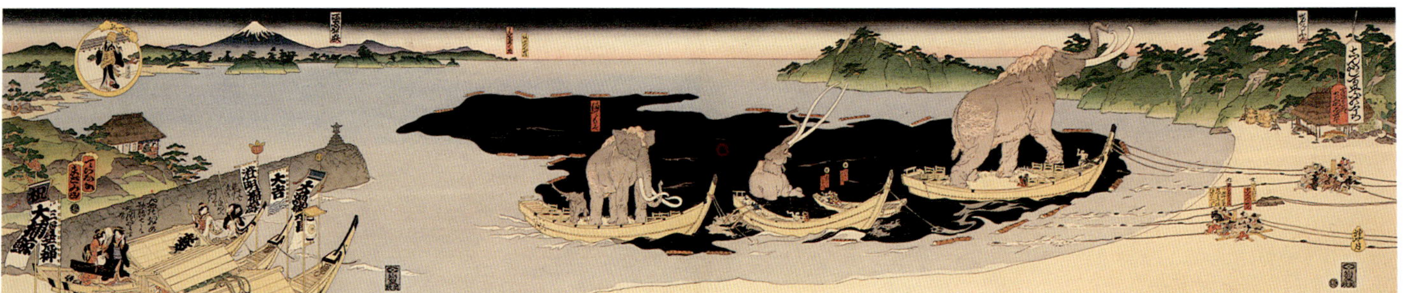

Fig. 9. *New Views of Mt. Fuji/La Brea Tar Pits and Pleasure Boats*, 1975, watercolor on paper, 11 × 55 inches, private collection.

incongruous bits of imagery lend a spark of humor to the narrative and conjure up a vision of women walking gaily along, munching on hamburgers and fries.

Hamburger and Chopsticks (fig. 7) and *Self-Portrait* (fig. 8) are lyrical still lifes possessing many of the same qualities as *Tokyo Ginza Shuffle.* Irony pervades. In the first painting, a hamburger and chopsticks, an unlikely combination, have been placed carefully on the ground beneath a flowering cherry tree. In the second still life, *Self-Portrait* (a portrait of the artist appears in a cartouche), a traditional bamboo broom, used to "sweep" the ground of a Japanese garden, and a partially eaten American hamburger create a similarly incongruous effect. In these works Teraoka quietly raises the issue of the slow contamination of the environment by the refuse produced by this American fad.

The theme of man's pollution of the environment grew increasingly prominent in Teraoka's paintings during the second half of the 1970s. Perhaps his strongest commentary on the materialistic business community that brought mass pollution to Japan is the series *New Views of Mount Fuji/La Brea Tar Pits* (figs. 9, 10). With acerbic wit Teraoka invented a narrative in which Japanese businessmen decide to purchase the La Brea Tar Pits and move them to Japan as an amusement park. A Japanese whaling fleet, in need of employment because it has slaughtered all the whales, transports the new acquisition. Teraoka chose the La Brea Tar Pits because of their intrinsic relationship to the natural geography of Los Angeles; Japan has no such symbol of its prehistoric past that he could draw on.

In the painting *La Brea Tar Pits and Pleasure Boats* (fig. 9), Teraoka depicted the tar pits as a huge oil slick being floated to Iwashijima Island from Los Angeles. Small figures in a frenzy of activity dot the landscape. Typical of Teraoka's satirical narratives are the Japanese inscriptions in the cartouches, which narrate the scene, criticizing the Japanese who permitted and aided the debasement. Workers on shore haul in long ropes that lead to boats carrying huge plastic mammoths. Someone in charge says, "Gokurōsan," thanking the workers for their hard work. A woman interjects, "Let's get ready," while a second announces, "Listen, everybody, this dumb thing is supposed to make a lot of money." On the opposite shore are traditional pleasure boats, symbols of the joy the Japanese people take in communing with nature. This is only a partial interpretation of the scene; as usual, Teraoka leaves little unexplained for the viewer capable of deciphering his many clues. (Teraoka would return to the satirical narrative in the 1980s to focus on the consequences of the Japanese tourist's infatuation with Hawaii's Hanauma Bay.)

In still another painting from the series, *La Brea Tar Pits Amusement Park* (fig. 10), the viewer is treated to a Disney-like ecological nightmare. Teraoka contained his subject within a large circle framed with an elaborate brocade design and set against churning waves. Here is the first expression of Teraoka's great love and concern for the sea, which will itself become a

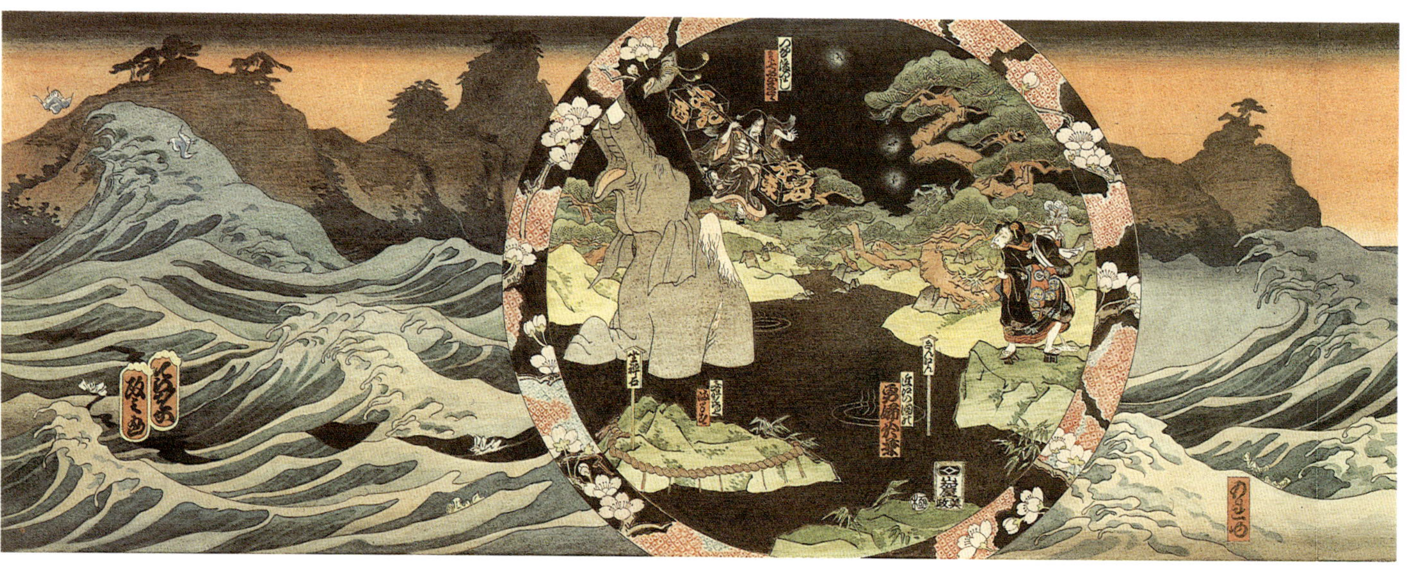

Fig. 10. *New Views of Mt. Fuji/La Brea Tar Pits Amusement Park* (detail), 1979, watercolor on paper, 11 × 55 inches, collection of Carl and Aviva Covitz, Los Angeles.

subject in the 1980s. Within the circular composition a huge mammoth sinks into a dark mass of tar, his trunk, high in the air, providing an anchor for a tightrope. A fierce-looking Kunisada-type beauty stands on the opposite shore, holding another rope between her teeth, her sharp, jutting jaw accentuated by the rope loop. Teraoka himself, dressed in Japanese robes, walks precariously down the tightrope, balancing two boxes on his shoulders. The boxes are marked "tō" (East) and "zai" (West). The scene cleverly parodies Teraoka's own cultural balancing act in real life. The struggling geisha, perhaps a satirical reference to Japan's feminists, holds the rope tautly between her teeth, golf clubs flung over one shoulder, and carries the inscription, "Yūfu Okame" (Brave Woman, Okame). Throughout the series Teraoka delights in poking fun at the Japanese, whether the shortcomings are traditional ones ("Don't pee in the tar pits") or more universal traits, such as greed.

Another series in the *New Views of Mount Fuji* set departs from the tar pit theme and focuses on a number of different subjects. In the well-known *Sinking Pleasure Boat* (fig. 11), which has been compared to Gericault's grim *The Raft of the Medusa*, Teraoka's earthy humor is given full play. One of the men in the sinking boat, bent over to expose his bare backside, is expelling gaseous fumes, releasing characters that suggest specific sounds of "breaking wind." Nearby, a woman holds her nose and is identified as "smelling woman." Teraoka's disarming earthiness is not without Japanese precedent. Narrative scrolls as early as the twelfth century depict the crudely humorous *He-gassen* (The Fart Battle). The scrolls served as models for paintings on the same gaseous subject that survive from the ukiyo-e school of the nineteenth century. A long handscroll by

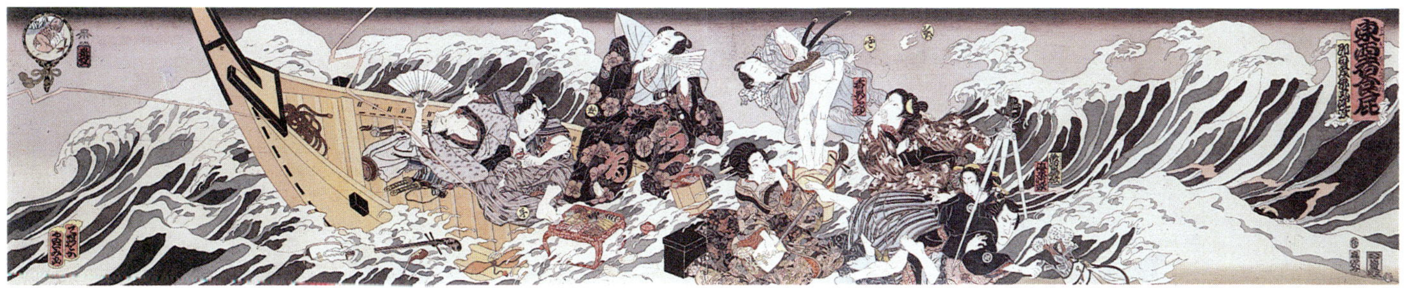

Fig. 11. *New Views of Mt. Fuji/Sinking Pleasure Boat*, 1976–77, watercolor on paper, 11 × 55 inches, collection of Dr. Michael Bléger, Los Angeles.

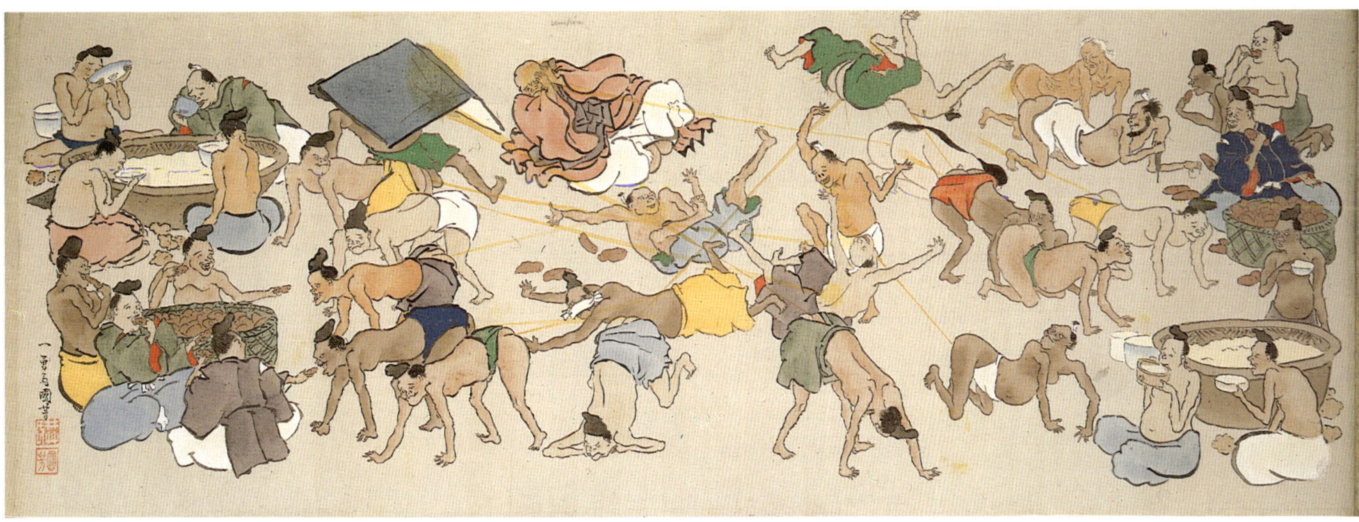

Fig. 12. Utagawa Kuniyoshi (attr.), *He-Gassen* (The Fart Battle) (detail), 1810, ink and color on silk, 10 3/4 × 102 1/4 inches, Honolulu Academy of Arts, gift of David W. Hall.

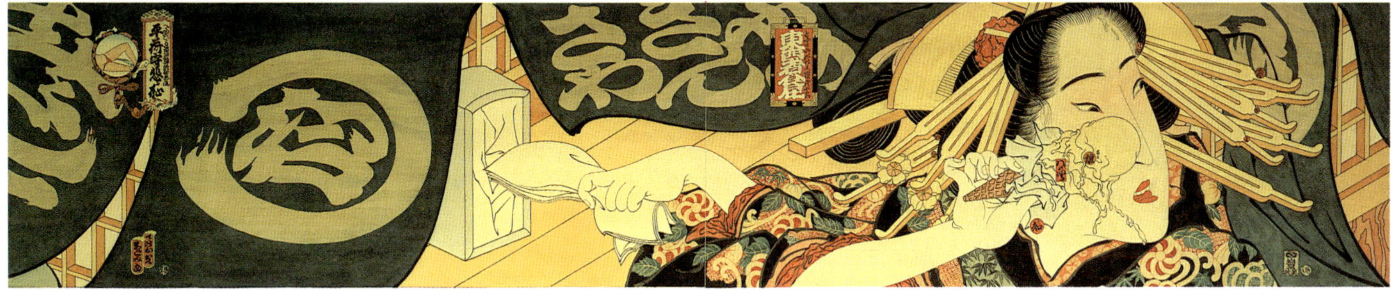

Fig. 13. *31 Flavors Invading Japan/French Vanilla IV*, 1979, watercolor on paper, 11 × 55 inches, collection of Marie Chun, Calabasas, California.

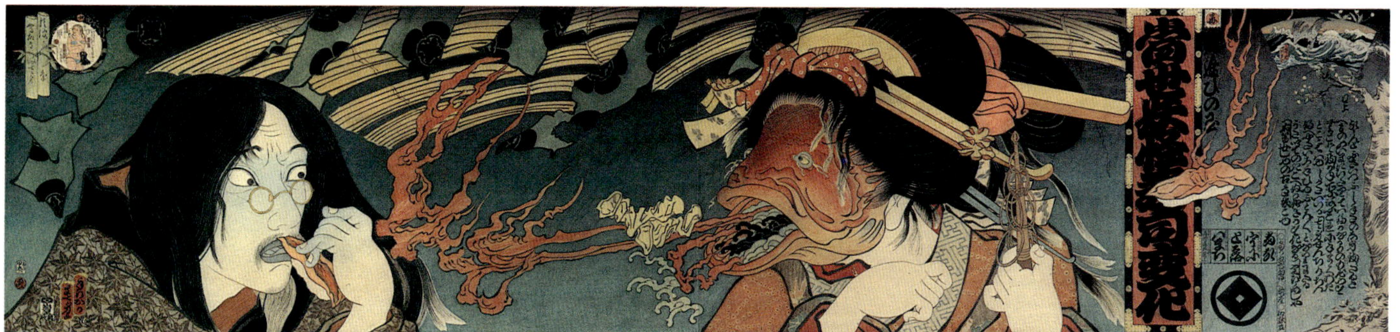

Fig. 14. *Los Angeles Sushi Ghost Tales/Fish Woman and the Artist I*, 1979, watercolor on paper, 13 × 55 inches, collection of the artist.

Kuniyoshi (fig. 12) is a gross retelling of the *He-gassen* and is part of the wealth of legend that gives even Teraoka's art a "traditional" endorsement.

Between 1977 and 1979 Teraoka painted the major series *31 Flavors Invading Japan*, which consists of seven paintings. In *French Vanilla IV* (fig. 13), a composition with erotic overtones similar to the earlier *Geisha and Tattooed Woman*, a Kunisada-type courtesan, overadorned with haircombs, holds a melting ice-cream cone. Teraoka wryly identifies the flavor as French vanilla, adding the term *tare*, or "drip," in Edo-period writing. But *tare* can also be pronounced *dare*, meaning "who" or "whose." The second character, *shiru*, which means "to know" and carries the alternate connotation of "juice," adds another layer of meaning. With these cryptic words Teraoka suggests that the direction of Japan's cultural attitudes defies prediction. The woman's facial expression suggests anxiety; sweat is breaking out on her brow, and she grabs napkins, an erotic confection, from a dispenser. A cartouche near her reads, "Comparing things, East and West; East-West people eat smelly food," a comment on another kind of pollution.

Teraoka's art took a more serious turn in his last series of the 1970s, *Los Angeles Sushi Ghost Tales*. In *Fish Woman and the Artist I* (fig. 14) a ghost appears before Masami Teraoka himself and warns him of the poisoned sushi he is about to eat. Ghosts in Japan are traditionally depicted as jealous women; however, here Teraoka has given his ghostly courtesan the face of a dead fish, reminiscent of the half-human, half-animal creatures of the ukiyo-e artist Utagawa Kuniyoshi, to whom Teraoka has repeatedly looked for inspiration. From the fish-woman's mouth spew forth ocean pollution and eerie flames. The effect is gross, disturbing, and yet fascinating. The setting is the stage of a noh play, and the theatricality of the scene is emphasized by a long description of the scene and its sound effects. Presented as if part of an actual playbill, the explanation begins: "In East and West we meet to enjoy all kinds of food, but today we cannot feel relaxed about eating properly. The curtain is going up now—here we go." Next to this narration appears a menu of polluted delicacies, with which any kind of cancer is offered free.

MASAMI TERAOKA IN HAWAII

Although Teraoka has been widely exhibited throughout America, the artist regards his exhibition of 1979, held at the Whitney Museum of American Art in New York, to be the most important one of his career. This trailblazing show, comprising twenty-two works of art, included some of the artist's finest paintings up to that time. The following year the exhibition traveled to the Newport Harbor Art Museum and the Fine Arts Museums of San Francisco in California and to the Honolulu Academy of Arts in Hawaii, giving the artist enormous exposure. As Teraoka suggests, the exhibition tour was a turning point in his life; after this time he expanded his artistic vocabulary and extended the scope of his vision. His trip to Honolulu to attend the opening at the Honolulu Academy of Arts, moreover, resulted in the move of his studio from smog-ridden Los Angeles to the spectacular coastline of Waimanalo Beach on Oahu's east shore, some twenty-five miles outside of Honolulu. "I am surrounded by a beautiful environment and it has deeply affected my art. Nature has served as my inspiration for the last eight years, and I am preoccupied with the beauty of the ocean—its waves, its turbulence; the spectacular moss-covered mountains that seem to rise to the sky, clouded with mists of great delicacy, are forever in my thoughts." Up to this time, Teraoka's lusty art had been primarily one of social protest against a world gone mad. Hawaii was to soften the hard edge of his criticism and his brush as Teraoka submerged himself in a deep and abiding love of nature. In this his Japanese background played a fundamental role. The pure landscape became a subject in and of itself.

Teraoka's preoccupation with turbulent water dates back to the 1970s. In *New Views of Mount Fuji/Waterfall Contemplation II* (fig. 15), he illustrates man's littering and waste in a tour-de-force composition. A waterfall, seemingly frozen in time, virtually dominates the scene, yet this is not a pure landscape but a narrative. A samurai, about to commit suicide, stares into the abyss. His sword rests on his ubiquitous golf bag and signposts announce, "No Smoking," "Not Allowed in Garden," and "No Littering." Over the last sign Teraoka has draped the black necktie of the last victim to commit suicide, the ultimate in ironic litter. Kleenexes and condoms float among the rapids and rocks—condom is here spelled phonetically, with the characters *kon* (this), *do* (time), and *umu* (birth), another twist of Teraoka's melancholy humor, raising the specter of an unwanted child, not to mention defective merchandise.

The works in this series recall the expressionistic art of Katsushika Hokusai's (1760–1849) famous waterfall series, or certain atmospheric landscapes of Kunisada or Keisai Eisen (1790–1848). Teraoka rendered his superbly controlled watercolors with an exaggerated calligraphic line typical of the woodblock medium, but he achieved it with a technical drawing pen rather than a brush, since the hard line of the pen comes closer to the quality of a woodblock line. Teraoka's woodblock illusion is yet another

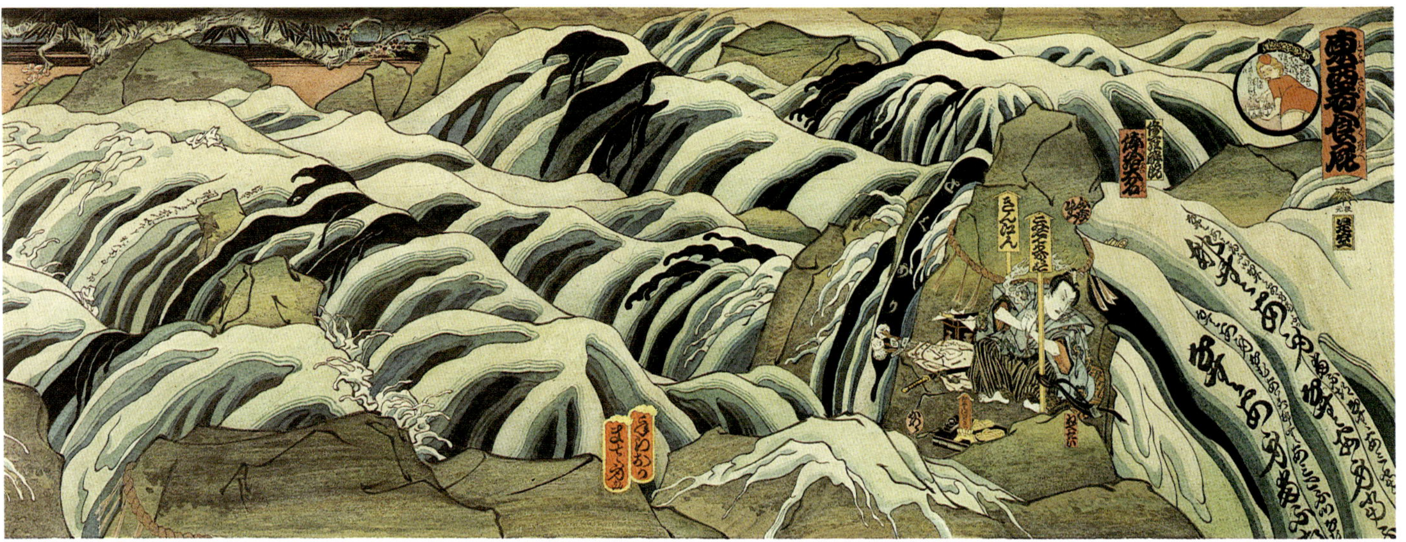

Fig. 15. *New Views of Mt. Fuji/Waterfall Contemplation II* (detail), 1979, watercolor and silkscreen on paper, 11 × 55 inches, collection of Herbert Solomon, Albany, California.

ironic twist: the original ukiyo-e print process attempted to reproduce inexpensively the calligraphic brush line of master artists. With tongue in cheek, Teraoka reversed the process.

Teraoka's more recent works, however, rely on the subtle modulation of line. For small areas he prefers a Western brush, but for large lines he has revived the traditional Japanese brush because of its capacity to create thick-thin calligraphic accents. Hand in hand with the introduction of a true brush line, his paintings have become much larger in size, and he has adopted the folding screen (*byōbu*), a traditional painting format unique to Japan. Furthermore, although most of Teraoka's paintings are pure watercolor, with black linear outlines rendered with watercolor lampblack (warmed with alizarin crimson), Teraoka also has experimented with traditional sumi ink. In the large painting entitled *Waves/Waimanalo Beach* (cat. no. 16), we see the spectacular results in a charged transparent composition of great vitality and freshness, in which man and pollution have been set aside in favor of the awesome beauty that nature alone can provide. In this sumi watercolor Teraoka worked directly on the large surface without a sketch or independent drawing as a guide. The results have never been more spontaneous or pleasing, and the calligraphic brush line virtually sings as ocean waves dance their way across the painting. The rich inks, moreover, add definition to the transparent blues of his delicate watercolor. Here Teraoka is not attempting to emulate the woodblock's layered flat color and graphically controlled line. Instead, he has moved toward the marvelously controlled, yet spontaneous brush line of Japanese ink painting. All that is left to remind one of Teraoka's debt to the ukiyo-e world are two black cartouches containing his signature, rendered in the style of Kunisada, and a traditional censorship seal reading "kiwame." The results are not as exacting as in other works, but his brush is guided by an identical spirit, one that springs from Japanese traditions that Teraoka alone seems able to make fresh again.

With his insatiable curiosity about all varieties of human and artistic experience, it is not surprising that the artist returned to the subject of erotica in the 1980s. Teraoka's preoccupation with sex stems from a deep-seated concern with male and female roles in human sexuality, a subject that was also of great interest to the Japanese from at least the Kamakura period (1185–1333) onward. Indeed, the earliest extant erotic scroll in Japan, *Chigo no sōshi* (Catamites scroll), dated in inscription to 1321 and kept at Sambō-in at the Daigo Temple in Kyoto, would be registered as a Cultural Property by the Japanese government if not for the fact that it deals exclusively with pederasty. The earliest recorded erotic scroll, *Yobutsu Kurabe*, depicted a court-sponsored phallic contest. Ascribed to Abbot Toba Sōjō (1053–1140), the scroll is known in a number of later but reliable copies. The scroll told the story of an imperial contest in which the more vigorous nobles displayed their phallic splendors to be measured by judges. Court ladies were permitted to watch in concealment and later to challenge the winners. During the Edo period many ukiyo-e artists designed erotic prints (*shunga*) based on medieval scrolls belonging to the aristocracy. In short, precedent for erotic subjects in traditional Japanese art is well established from at least the twelfth century.

In Teraoka's erotic art one finds the ultimate in satire of the savagery, joy, bitterness, frenzy, and ridiculousness of sex. The paintings in the *Wave* series that deal with erotic subject matter are all seemingly based on illustrations by Hokusai in the three-volume erotic book *Kinoe no Komatsu* (Young Pine Shoots), published sometime around 1814. In compositions startling in both execution and content, Teraoka, following Hokusai's lead, depicted a large octopus or giant squid ravishing a young Japanese girl with adroit cunnilingus. The results are even more bizarre than Hokusai's conception, and one comes away with the feeling that these works by Teraoka are neither comic nor pornographic. They are, rather, fantasies of passionate proportion (cat. nos. 6–9).

Not all of Teraoka's watercolors of this period dismiss the subject of Japan's collision course with Western culture. Along with its computers and cars, Japan has been sending its tourists to the West as well. Earlier in his career, Teraoka chronicled the tomfoolery at Venice Beach, California, and in the 1980s Teraoka turned his wry brush to painting the shores of Hawaii, populated with Japanese tourists. In Teraoka's words: "Hanauma Bay is one of the most popular tourist spots on Oahu. It is a tropical fish sanctuary where tourists love to snorkel. I often see Japanese tourists come over here with video equipment. They might have brought it from home or rented it from stores in Waikiki . . . whatever moves they make, they want to record on tape. Wherever they stop, their time is short, and they have to split for the next attraction. Since they are on this super-fast tour of Hawaii they never have time to see very much."

Teraoka has produced an entire series relating to this type of tourist at Hanauma Bay, including *Wikiwiki Tour* (cat. no. 1), *Video Rental II* (cat. no. 2), *Samurai Camera Crew and Blowhole II* (cat. no. 3), *Rōnin Samurai* (cat. no. 4), and *Catfish Zen Monk* (cat. no. 5). In *Samurai Camera Crew and Blowhole II*, Teraoka has chosen the same measurements as a large video screen. He treats the painting as if it were a kabuki theater poster, using ideograms to proclaim that his friends Kazuo Kadonaga and Ann Page are playing the starring roles, in which they struggle under the weight of snorkeling gear. As Gerald Haggerty notes (Jacksonville, 1983), "The fins and mask make up beautiful black shapes which suggest Edo costumes; the watery setting, a 'floating Hawaiian World,' recalls that of Utamaro's pearl divers a century and a half ago."

Masami's allusions do not stop with the pictorial itself. The title of the series, *Hanauma Bay*, utilizes a mixture of symbolic characters and phonetic kana. *Ha* is the symbol for wave, while *u* is the symbolic character for clouds, or if extended, nature. Thus, singularly appropriate to this particular bay, *ha* and *u* together carry a secondary meaning, "the way of nature."

Although deeply affected by the natural majesty and serenity of Hawaii, Teraoka's social conscience was roused once again when the reality of Acquired Immune Deficiency Syndrome (AIDS) struck close to home. In 1986, while visiting New York, he learned that a friend's newborn child had contracted AIDS as the result of a blood transfusion. Shocked by the news and by the horrible fear that was soon to grip the world, Teraoka felt compelled to turn his acid brush to the perils and weaknesses of an unsound society.

In his series on AIDS Teraoka depicts the wrath that nature sometimes sees fit to bestow on mankind, and by treating AIDS as yet another form of world debasement, he dramatically extends his biting satire on pollution. In the superb painting *Fish Woman and the Artist I* (fig. 14), from the 1979 series *Los Angeles Sushi Ghost Tales*, Teraoka's narrative suggests that anyone who eats polluted raw fish is destined to become a ghost. In his view, the same is true if one engages in unsafe sex.

Drawing upon the theatricality and playbill-like presentation of the earlier series, Teraoka set about to produce his now-famous *American Kabuki/ Oishiiwa* (cat no. 18), a watercolor on paper mounted as a four-panel folding screen. As in the past, he drew upon the resources of Japanese tradition, but instead of selecting the grossly graphic disease scrolls of the fourteenth century as his inspiration, Teraoka disguised his message by using the ghost legends and conventions of kabuki theater, which, like ukiyo-e, are filled with innuendo and symbolism. The overall effect startles the viewer, evoking curiosity, repugnance, and wonder at the painting's layers of illusion and the sheer beauty of its execution.

Masami Teraoka continues to synthesize aspects of Japanese and American culture in ukiyo-e style paintings of superbly rendered line and delicate washes that transcend time or place to say much about our world today and its values. His lusty art remains one of social protest and social ridicule, an art that exposes the follies, weaknesses, and wrongs of our society. In Teraoka's best work, keen satire produces the love-hate reaction that hits at the very soul of creating. Teraoka remains an omnipresent viewer of mankind, now being forced to examine the most sinister plague of our age, or perhaps of any age. Teraoka continues to remind us, with a biting wit as merciless as Voltaire's, that art, like the life it reports, has myriad facets. Now more than ever his art has an urgency to communicate.

1

HANAUMA BAY SERIES

WIKIWIKI TOUR

1982, watercolor on paper, 21 3/8 × 77 in.
Space Gallery, Los Angeles

This fantastic narrative combines acerbic wit with penetrating social commentary on the Japanese tourist in Hawaii. In narrative style it harkens back to the *La Brea Tar Pits* series, although the setting is now Hanauma Bay, a fish preserve Teraoka considers as unique to Hawaii as the tar pits are to Los Angeles.

As in a traditional scroll, the narrative reads from right to left. A red cartouche on the far right obliquely identifies the scene as "Fūzoku Kurabe," which might best be translated as "manners and customs comparisons." Figures in a frenzy of activity dot the shoreline; the crater landscape of the bay rises in the background. A black and white cartouche presented in the style of a kabuki playbill (*banzuke*) provides the rules and regulations for the visiting Japanese tourist. It can be loosely translated: "Do's and Dont's for the tourist. Things to bring: golf clubs, digital watch, calculator, and of course the ubiquitous camera. Places to visit: the Bishop Museum, the Honolulu Academy of Arts, the Contemporary Arts Center [now The Contemporary Museum], the Restaurant Bueno Nalo, Hanauma Bay, the Royal Hawaiian Hotel in Waikiki, Sunset Beach, and Pali Lookout. Places to avoid: Waimanalo Beach, Waianae Beach. Additional advice: Be sure to lock the door of your rent-a-car."

The photographer of the scene, dressed as a kabuki actor, is identified in a small cartouche as the artist himself. He bends over, taking a picture of the curious samurai picnic. A standing woman, her long blonde hair flowing freely over her shoulders, aids him. A samurai guide, holding a rented video camera, a snorkel mask, and two pineapples, carries a tour flag which says, "The Least Expensive Tour Group." Nearby, in a cartouche, is the additional comment: "Discount Tour Group." Hilarious details fill the scene: the tourists drink pineapple juice; a digital watch alarm goes off. Someone says, "Get ready for Waikiki." A woman places leis across a picnic lunch box; seated next to the lunch box is a Japanese carpenter holding a T-square. A samurai, he looks lustfully after a Western woman riding a horse along the edge of the shore. In Edo-period parlance, when a man is attracted to a woman, the space between his upper lip and nose grows, an obvious reference to the male erection. The ruler, therefore, is present as a metaphor; the carpenter is measuring his own excitement. Another Japanese visitor plays in the sand, looking for seashells by a pine tree. Near the tree is a crab carrying a used condom; the implication is that one should take away used refuse and prevent the debasement of nature. Another crab, with the plastic container for a tampon, talks to a Japanese woman, asking her to take the container with the shells she collects. In the distance can be seen the mountains of Waimanalo; the famed Rabbit Island is nearby. At the top is a circular red cartouche with the characters for East and West. Finally, in a fan cartouche is a depiction of Griffith Park Observatory in Los

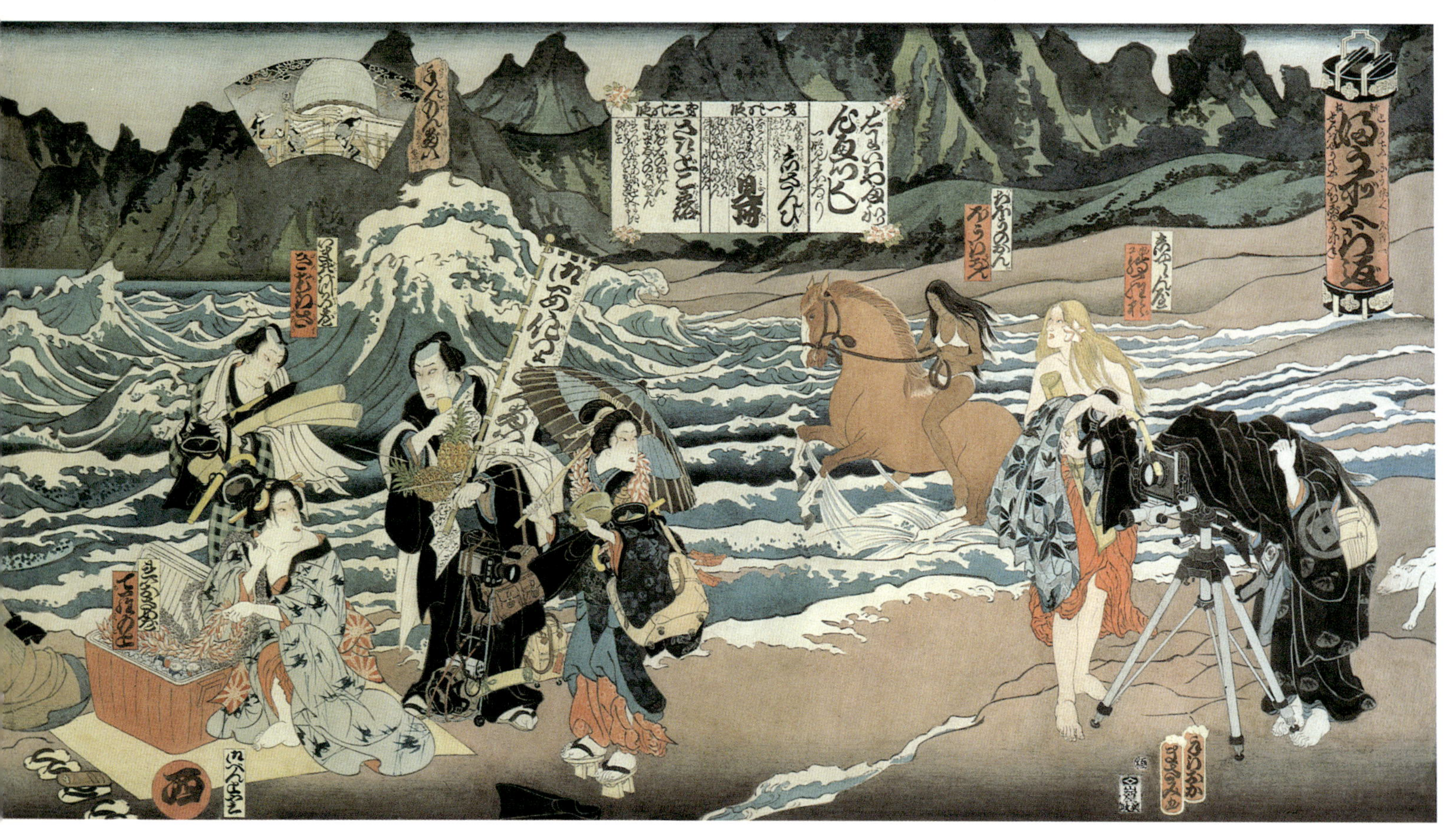

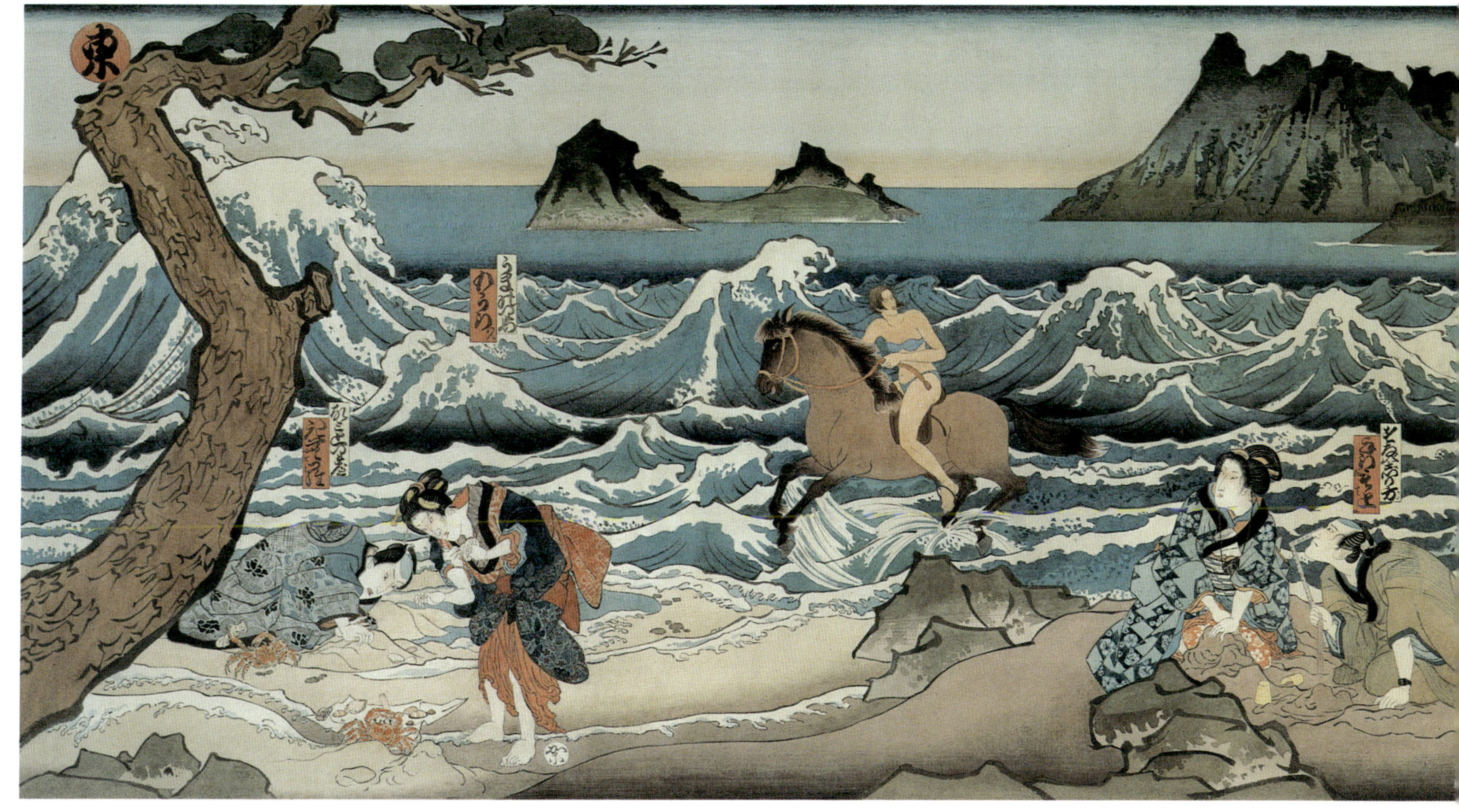

Angeles and an inscription suggesting that Japanese craftsmen should work on its repair, since some still do a quality job. (In 1982, at the time this painting was made, Griffith Park Observatory was in need of restoration.) Throughout the narrative, Teraoka includes cartouche inscriptions to identify the actors and their roles, as if this were a scene from kabuki. A wealth of carefully inserted, ironic commentary defines Teraoka's Voltaire-like satirism and his concern that both societies should do more to keep nature intact.

2

HANAUMA BAY SERIES

VIDEO RENTAL II

1984, watercolor on paper, 28 1/4 × 40 5/8 in.
Collection of Mr. and Mrs. Robert Marin, Los Angeles

In this imaginative narrative, based on a smaller composition, *Video Rental I*, Teraoka limited his color palette in order to stress the sudden cold rain that has caught two Japanese snorkelers as they photograph fish in the famed Hanauma Bay fish preserve. The Japanese script in the cartouche to the right and in the long inscription at the top of the painting illuminates the scene on many levels. The long vertical *tanzaku* cartouche to the right reads, "Ōisogi Hawaii ga meguri; oyogi no hito koma." Written in Japanese kanji with hiragana to assist pronunciation, this inscription translates, "A snapshot of swimming people in Hawaii." The scene shows a young samurai, holding a video camera, looking up at stormy clouds. Huddled next to him in the water is his wife, holding the video recorder and a samurai sword. Both figures are painted in the style of Kunisada. The contemporary dress and the snorkeling equipment are in sharp contrast to this traditional drawing style.

The dialogue above the figures explains the scene, which is titled "Ame," or rain, followed by "Hanauma Bay" in phonetic hiragana. The wife speaks, "My feet are freezing—let's get out of here. I can't take it any more." The samurai retorts, "Well, we just got here. I promised to take some footage of parrot fish. Would you mind waiting?" This is followed by a haiku poem, which translates, "The sound of rings of bubbles from fish competing for food." At the end of the narrative is a list of actors in the kabuki cast, for the entire scene is made to appear as if it were a theatrical poster, and even includes the Teraoka family crest. According to the inscription, the samurai role is played by Saburō Kimura, Teraoka's brother-in-law, and the wife is played by Yasue Kimura, his sister. An insert of a parrot fish completes the visual. An additional round cartouche shows a street in Waikiki with a brochure stand and a free guide to the activities of Hawaii—a reminder of the high speed "wikiwiki" tour that Japanese tourists endure.

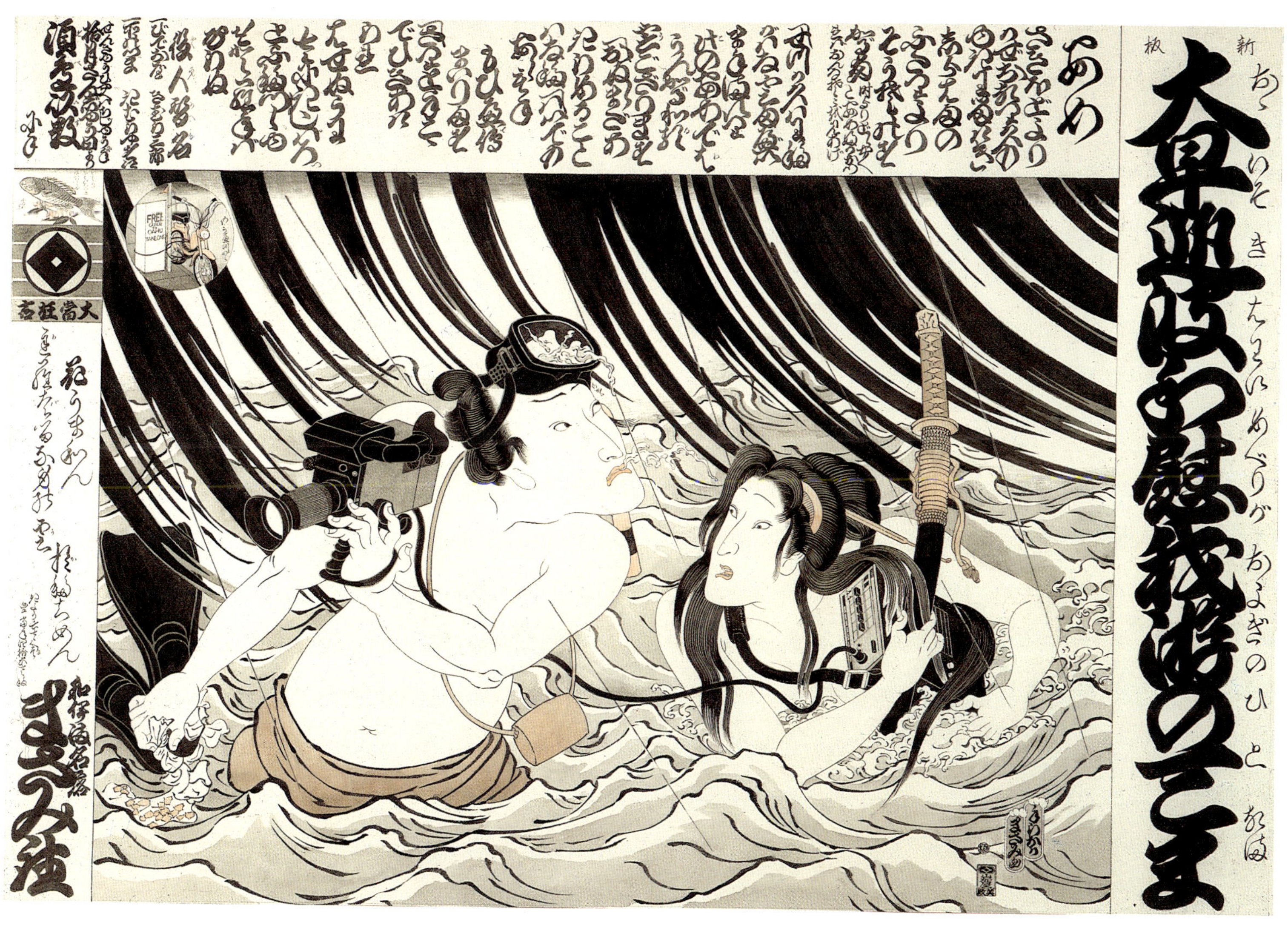
FREE

3

HANAUMA BAY SERIES

SAMURAI CAMERA CREW AND BLOWHOLE II

1982, watercolor on paper, 28 3/4 × 40 5/8 in.
Collection of Terry Rhodes, Midland, Texas

This fine painting is an early work from the *Hanauma Bay* series. Entitled in cartouche, "Shinban Hanauma Bay" (New Woodblock series, Hanauma Bay), Teraoka has employed specific kanji ideograms for the *ha* and *u* of the Hawaiian name. *Ha* carries the meaning of wave, and *u* carries the meaning clouds, or by extension, nature. The implication is that "this is the way of nature."

A samurai and his wife are photographing and snorkeling at Hanauma Bay. The wife, with camera, is ready to photograph two tropical fish that have risen to the surface. Around her neck is a plastic bag containing dog food or bread, used to attract the fish. She is identified in cartouche as Ann Page, an artist and a friend of Teraoka. The samurai is adjusting his snorkel equipment; water apparently has gotten under his face mask. Both of his flippers are snuggled close to his body under his left arm. The samurai is identified as Kazuo Kadonaga, also an artist-friend of Teraoka. To the left, in a vertical cartouche, the actor credits are given as well as the name of the series, a reminder to all that Teraoka is treating the series as scenes from a kabuki play. A fan cartouche in the upper left corner includes a design of a Caucasian woman, identified as Felice Matare, in diving gear. Teraoka's name is included in the usual Kunisada-style cartouche and also is given in the vertical cartouche on the right, along with the date of the composition (1982).

As in all of his compositions after the late 1970s, Teraoka here used a brush, preferring its greater flexibility over the technical pen. The limited color of the painting emphasizes the focus of the composition: the gigantic black forms of the samurai's huge flippers. This is the most turbulent scene in the series, with waves churning white from dashing against coral rocks.

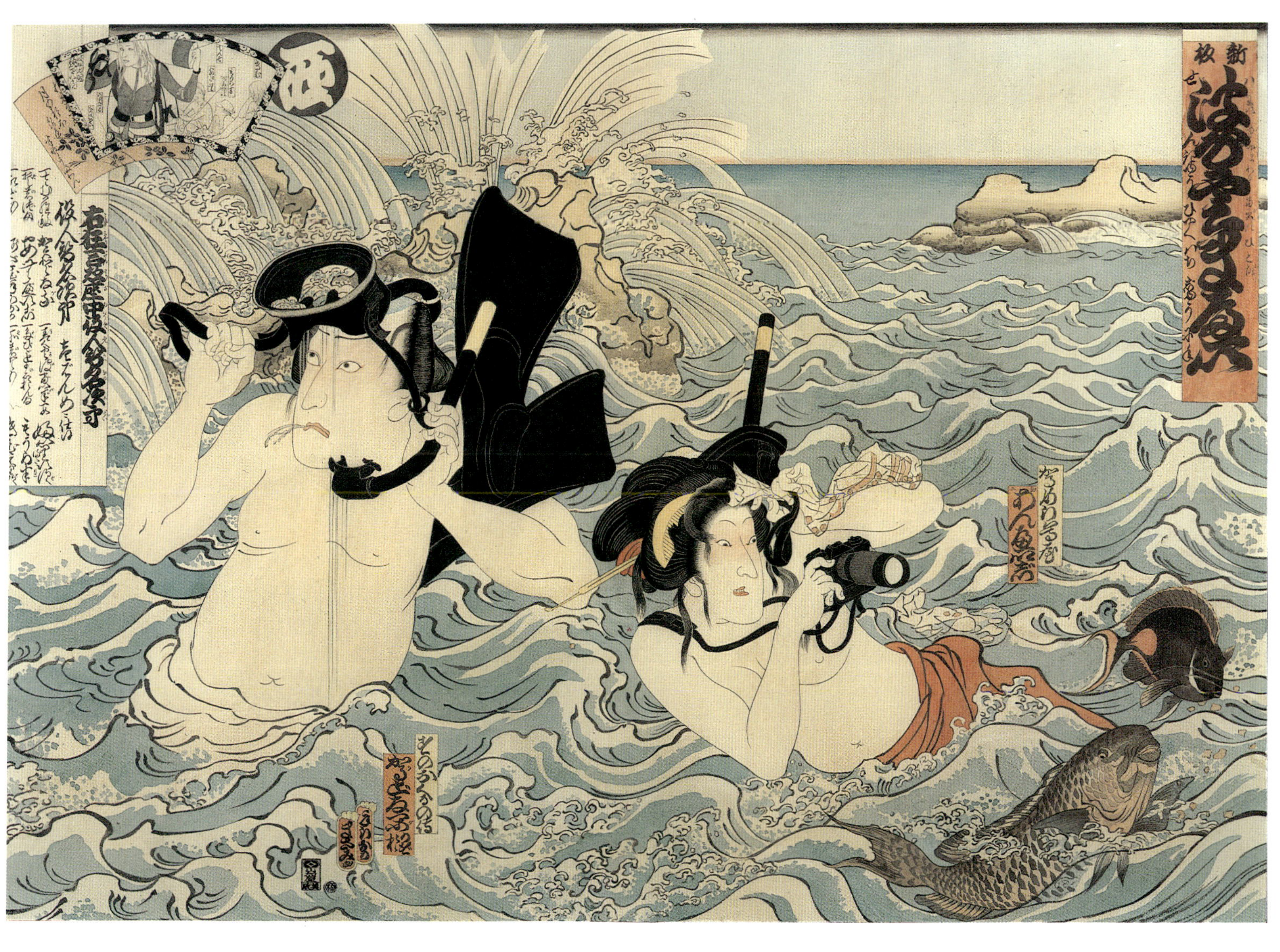

4

HANAUMA BAY SERIES
RŌNIN SAMURAI

1982, watercolor on paper, 28 3/4 × 40 5/8 in.
Space Gallery, Los Angeles

The Japanese title of this work makes no reference to the *rōnin* samurai depicted in the painting, which carries the inscription "Ō-atari Kyōgen no Space-za." "Kyōgen" refers to a kabuki or noh play interlude, and "Ō-atari" refers to a hit play. Loosely translated, the title, therefore, is "A Big Hit Kabuki Scene at the Space Theater."

Teraoka's archetypal blonde lady emerges from the water to inquire after a strange-looking samurai, depicted in a particularly grimacing *mie* (sustained pose), his eyes crossed and one arm outstretched in an awkward posture recalling the great kabuki prints of Kunisada made in the 1830s. In one hand he holds a round fan with a long bamboo handle. His snorkeling mask is raised over his head, and he has moved the rest of his equipment to either side of his face. He wears a black rubber suit, but beneath it can be seen a traditional Japanese tie-dye fabric. From his neck a traditional Japanese wallet (*saifu*) hangs loosely to his hip. In his outstretched left hand he holds a strange instrument that is giving off electrical shock impulses.

As in most of Teraoka's compositions, all is explained in a lengthy inscription that provides the dialogue: "The blonde lady inquires, 'I'm curious as to what you are doing.' The samurai replies, 'I'm looking for coins or lost articles.'" The commentary refers to the high unemployment rate in Japan in 1982. This proud samurai, of the masterless (*rōnin*) class, in this case unemployed, looks for metal trinkets, much as one of America's homeless might do in an attempt to survive. The dialogue continues, "The lady replies: 'Waikiki is much better than here.' The *rōnin* retorts, 'Yes, but the hotels are empty now.'"

The entire scene is beautifully painted with a combination of Japanese and Western brushes. The water is particularly convincing, although considerably simplified when compared with *Samurai Camera Crew and Blowhole II* (cat. no. 3). In this composition the usual Kunisada-style cartouches for Teraoka's name are included along with the traditional censorship (*kiwame*) seal. As usual, Teraoka's family crest appears as a publisher's mark.

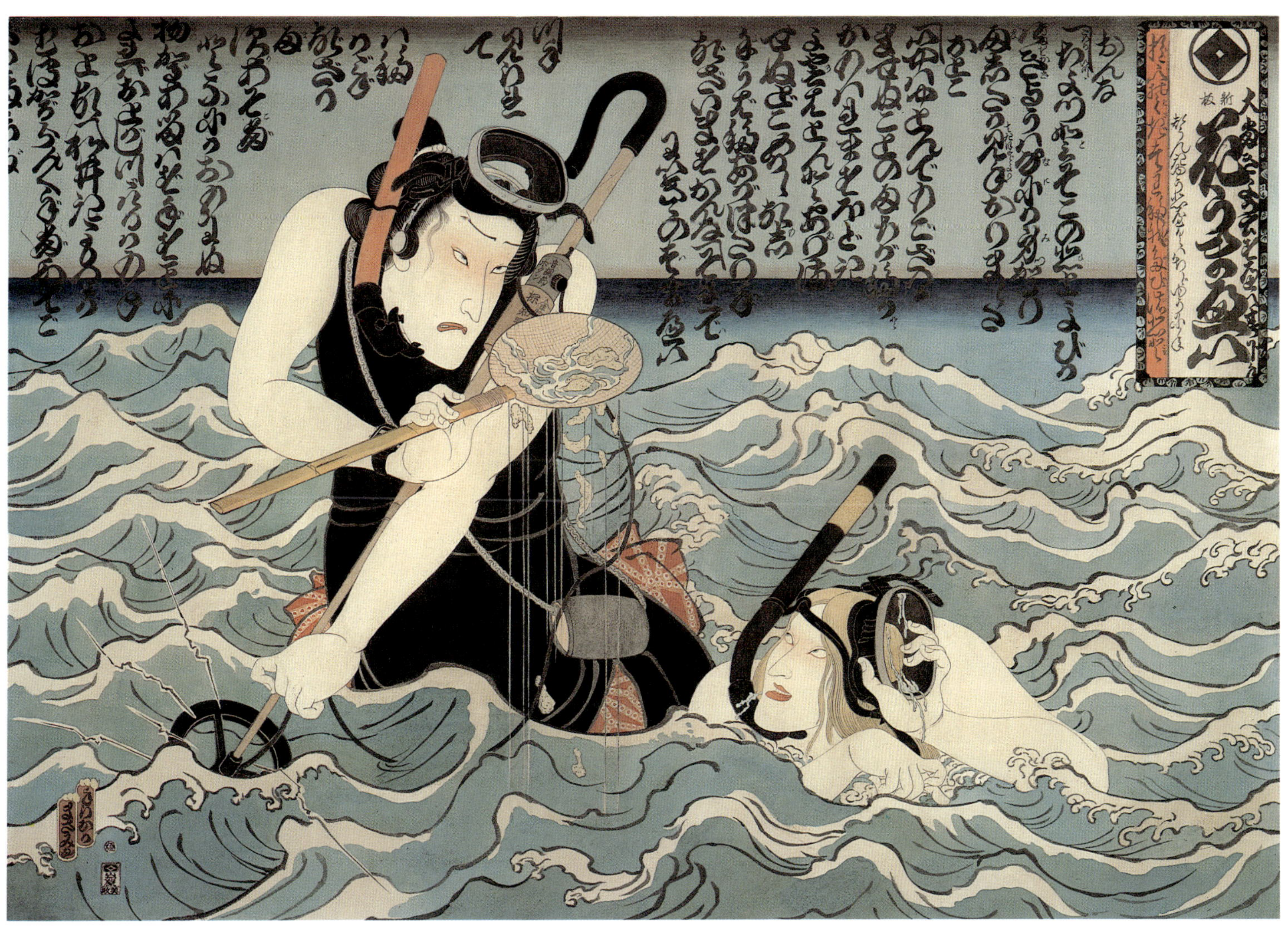

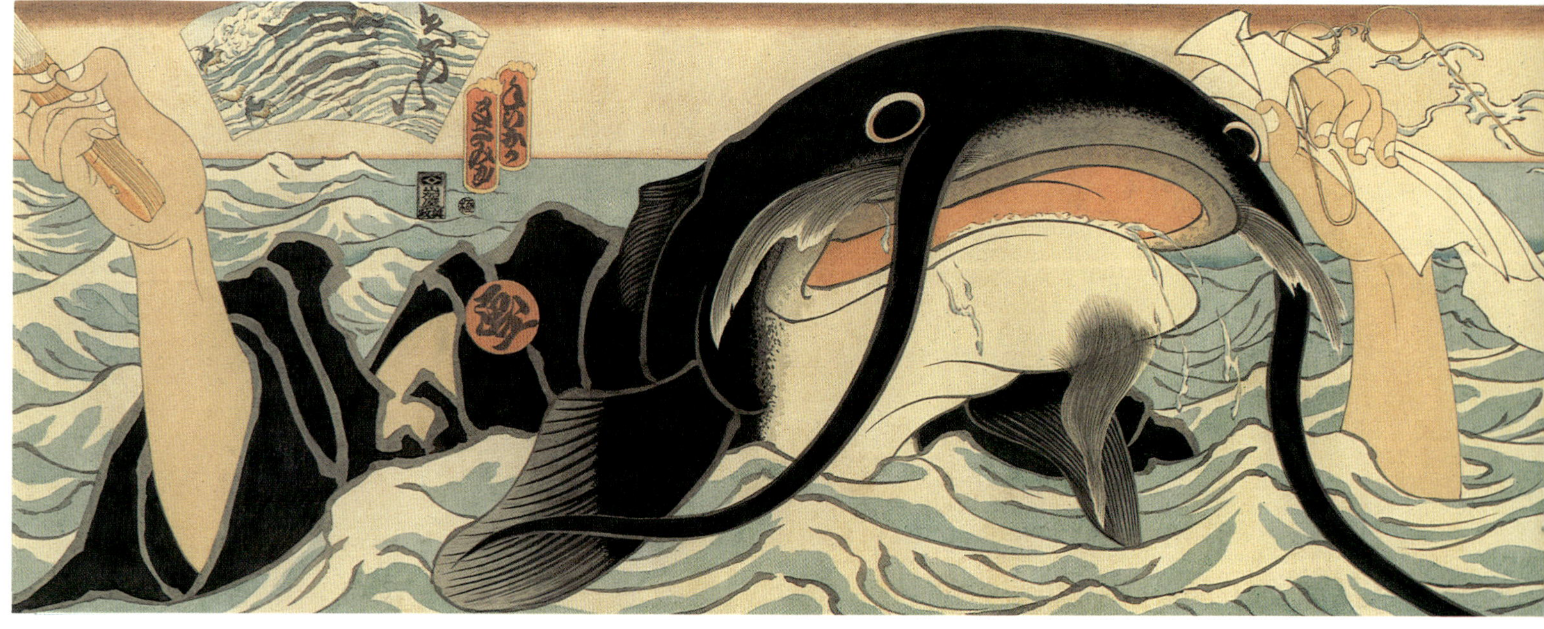

5

HANAUMA BAY SERIES

CATFISH ZEN MONK

1984, watercolor on paper, 13 × 55 in.
Space Gallery, Los Angeles

Teraoka has reverted to a horizontal composition for this particularly fantastic scene, in which he renders himself as a monk with the face of a catfish. We recognize Teraoka's formal kimono, his goatee, and his wire-rimmed glasses. He rises out of the water at Hanauma Bay, startling a swimmer, who spurts water from her mouth in disbelief. Teraoka holds a closed folding fan in his right hand; it is the type used by samurai as well as by kabuki actors to add emphasis to a declamation. In his left hand he holds his eyeglasses and a towel. Sweating because he has swum some distance, the catfish warns the Japanese tourist of a floating mine that might explode.

This topical painting makes reference to a bomb scare in South America. A fan cartouche reads "kirai," or dislike, and depicts water mines with birds (*chidori*) flying around them. Here Teraoka tells the world that if war escalates even a fish sanctuary as lovely as Hanauma Bay could be destroyed.

Teraoka has done a number of sketches utilizing the Kuniyoshi-like form of a catfish, which in Japanese legend is thought to be a prophet, or a psychic. In the catfish study *Hanauma Bay Series/Zen Catfish Monk*, a vertical sketch on paper executed in 1984, Teraoka, as a catfish, holds a mechanism used to detect earthquake tremors. He considers the fact that the American economy, like a huge mastodon, is going down as the government deficit goes up. In another sketch, Teraoka has depicted a catfish inventing a back stretcher; in another catfish portrait he portrays a nuclear holocaust. In still other catfish fantasies he has placed the psychic prophet at the Santa Monica Pier with the messages "death is imminent" and "there is no place to go."

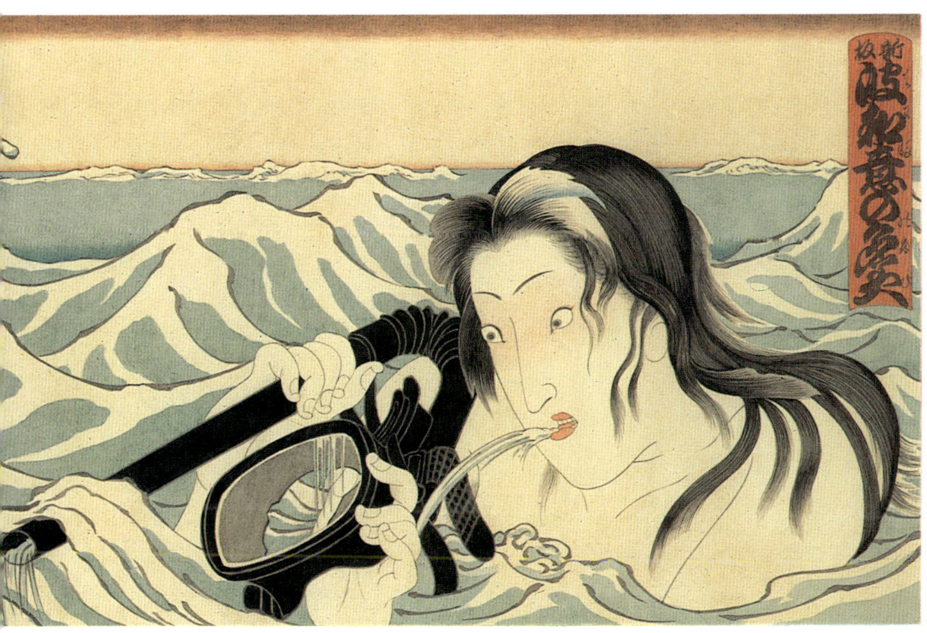

Not always is the catfish made to be the prophet of doom: in another more humorous series (a continuation of his earlier *Nude Venice Beach* series), Teraoka includes himself as a Zen monk catfish learning aerobic dancing. The catfish picture (*nama-zu*) affords the artist a particularly rich iconography by which he mocks the obsessions of mankind.

6

WAVE SERIES

TATTOOED WOMAN AT KANEOHE BAY I

1984, watercolor on paper, 14 1/2 × 21 1/2 in.
Collection of Jan and Joe Cobert

A scuba diver, tattooed with dragon motifs, is being ravaged by a giant octopus; the monster seems unusually lustful in its pursuit. In this painting we find Teraoka's genius at erotica fulfilled; it is a consummate work. Known also in a brush drawing, the painting (dated 1984 in the yellow cartouche in the top left corner) is thought to be the earliest in this unique series. The red cartouche carries the title "Woman and Giant Lunch Box." The inscription adds humor and wit to the fantasy: "The diver speaks: 'Please let me go, right now!' The octopus answers, 'No, I finally found a wonderful lunch, I won't let you go.'" The inscription ends with the statement "to be continued," as if the scene were an episode of a television serial.

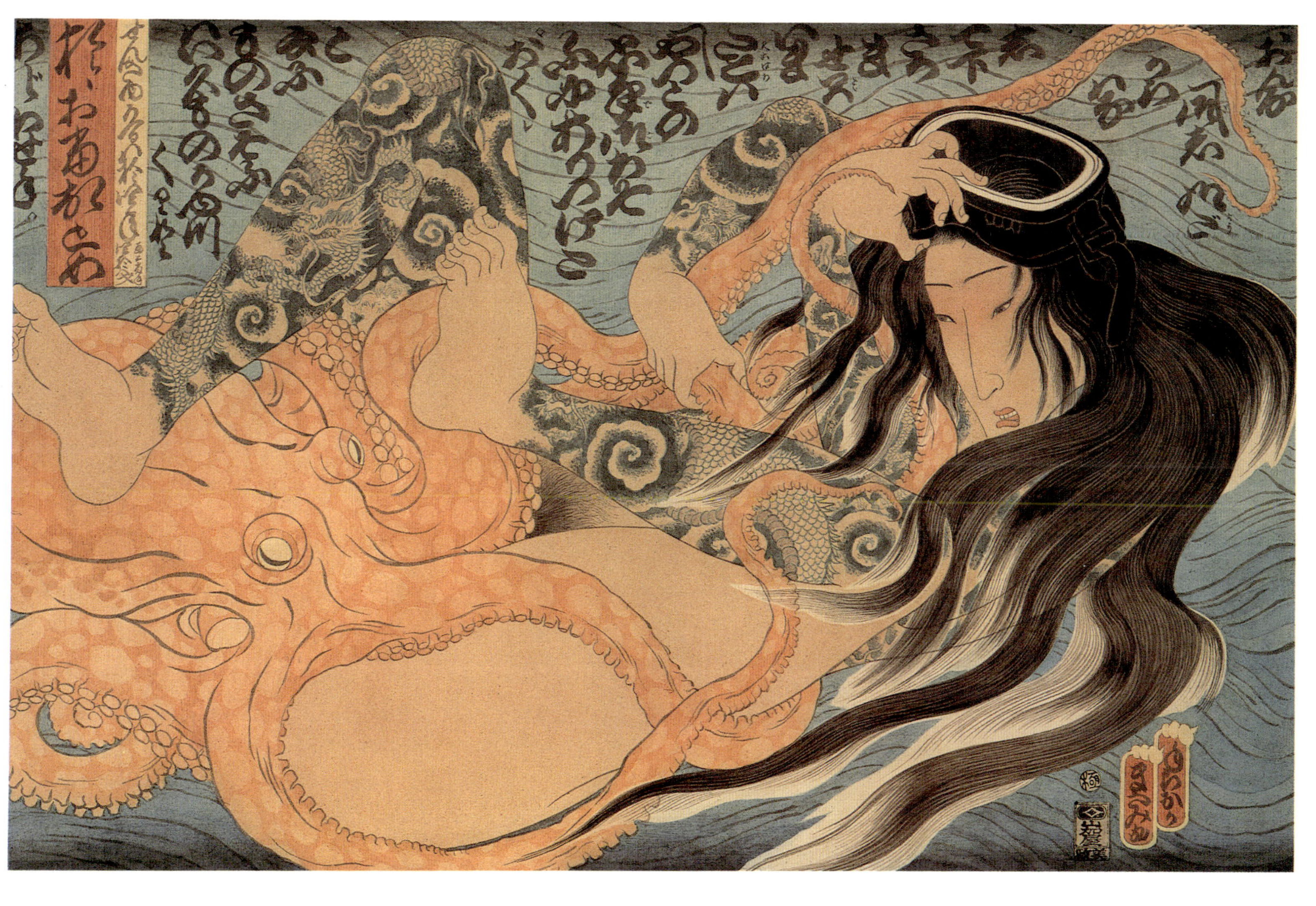

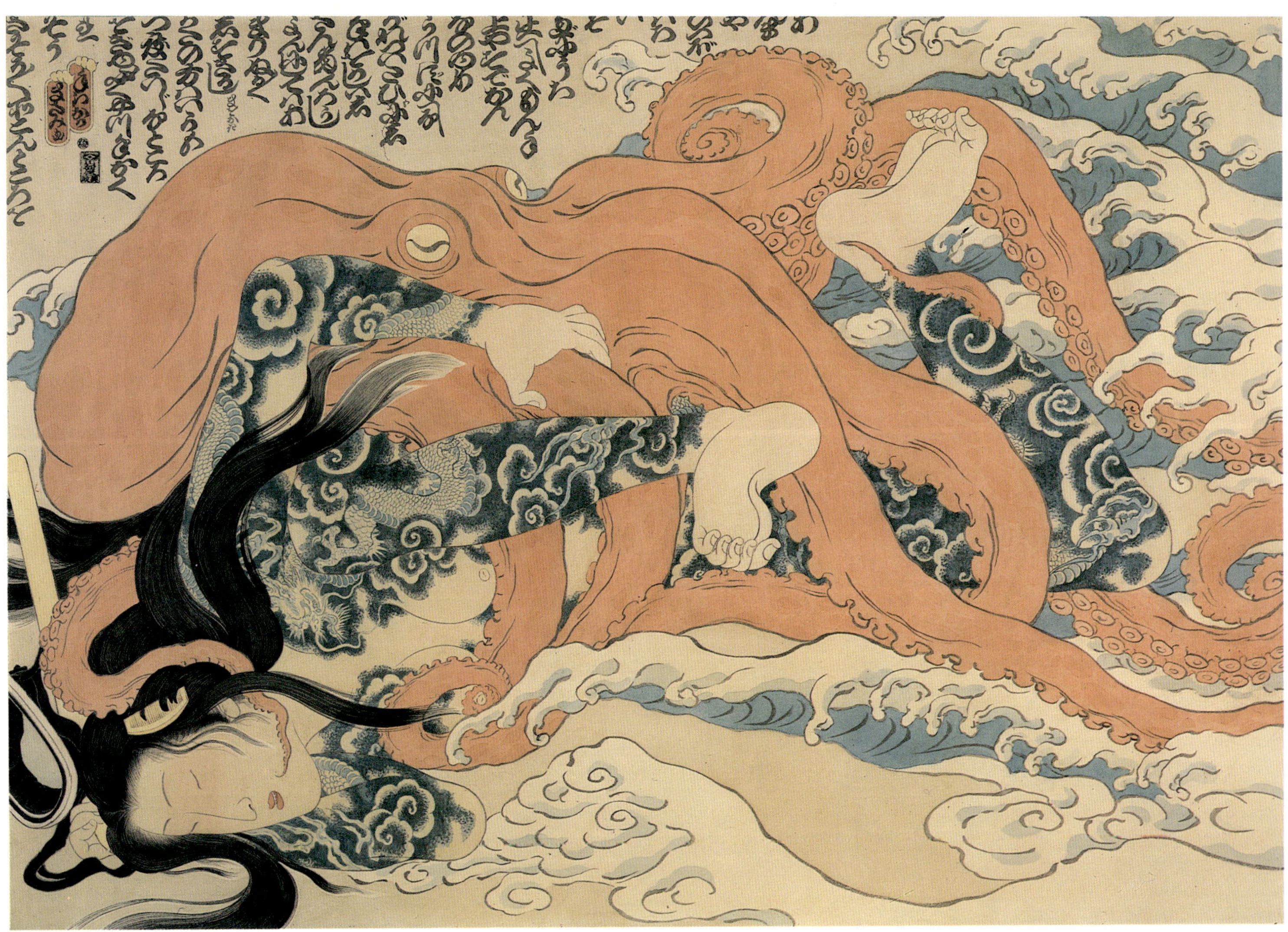

7

WAVE SERIES

TATTOOED WOMAN AT SANDY BEACH

1984, watercolor on paper, 28 3/4 × 40 5/8 in.
Space Gallery, Los Angeles

Regarded by many as the best erotic painting in the *Wave* series, *Tattooed Woman at Sandy Beach* was inspired by a tangled thick rope that Teraoka found while walking along Waimanalo Beach. Teraoka's fertile mind set to work, and a fantasy of passionate eroticism resulted. A tattooed woman is seen lying at the water's edge. Waves projecting long finger-like extensions seem to aid an octopus as it ravishes the young diver. Her legs are spread apart at an impossible angle, and one hand clutches a long tentacle of the passionate octopus as she attempts to guide it to a particularly sensitive part of her body. The inscription is revealing: "A tattooed woman falls asleep where the ocean meets the sandy beach. An old piece of drift rope tangles with her body, and she dreams that it is an octopus as the rope begins to caress her body. Finally she says, 'How strange! What is happening? From my head to my toe there is some slimy feeling. I didn't put suntan lotion on so why should I feel this way?'" Then she feels that "delightful pressure on her genitals. To be continued (*tsuzuku*)." In this dramatic and passionate painting, Teraoka succeeds in combining linear fluency with a rare evocative power.

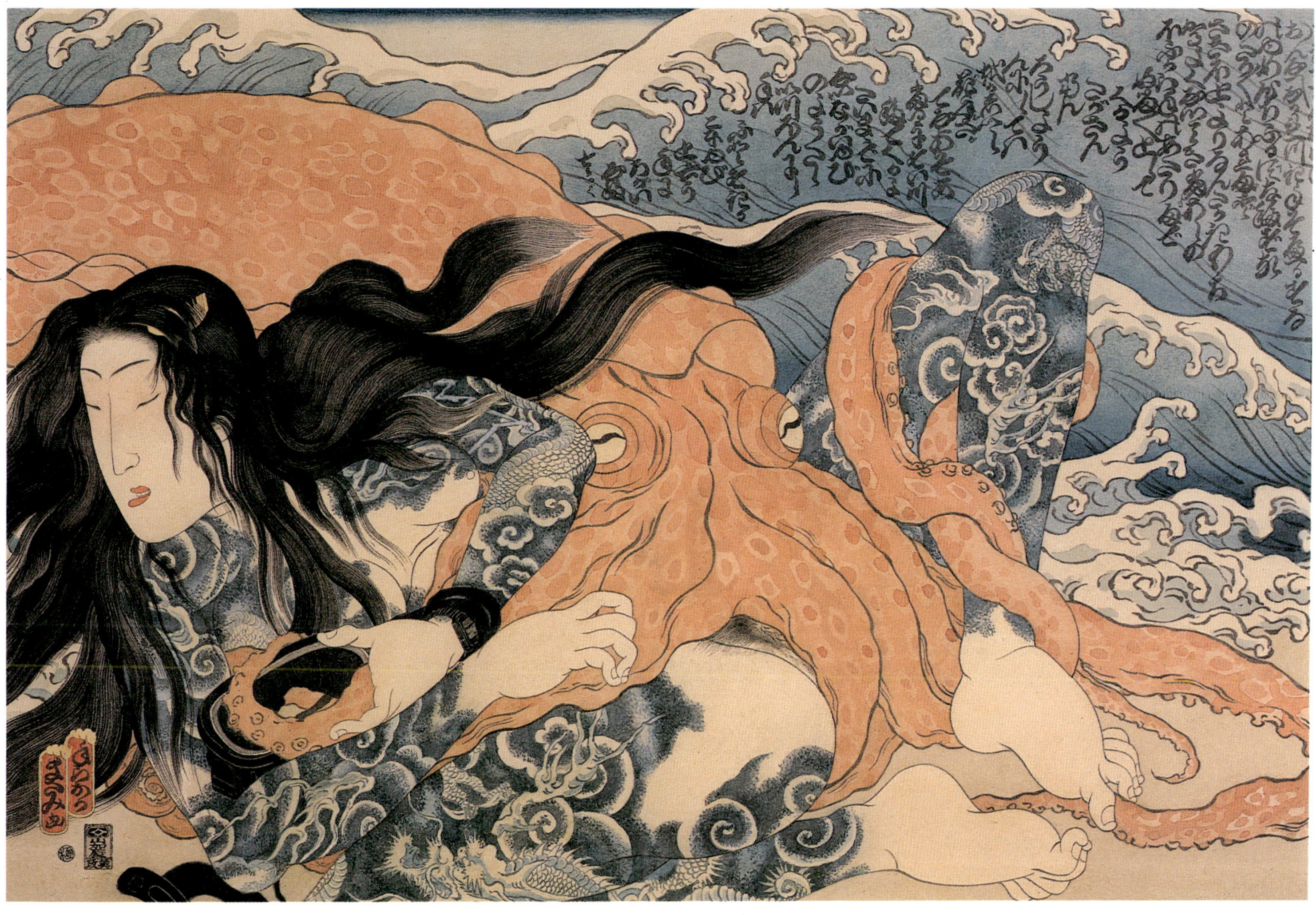

8

WAVE SERIES
TATTOOED WOMAN AT MAKAPUU BEACH

1984, watercolor on paper, 20 × 29 in.
Space Gallery, Los Angeles

This painting is a highly successful variant of *Tattooed Woman at Sandy Beach* (cat. no. 7) and underlines a sentiment common among Japanese gallants of the Edo period: giving a lady pleasure is more important than satisfying oneself. The lustful look of the tattooed protagonist suggests that she is nearing sexual climax. In her hand she holds a face mask, which wraps around her arm like the tentacles of the lustful monster. Its head is tucked between her open legs, in the act of devouring her genitals. The eyes of the giant squid express ecstasy.

The inscription confirms that this work is a variation of *Tattooed Woman at Sandy Beach*. Its narrative content differs only slightly in detail: "A woman is sunbathing at the beach and while sleeping a sliminess comes over her body. 'Is this my suntan lotion that feels so good?' she says. 'Hmm.'"

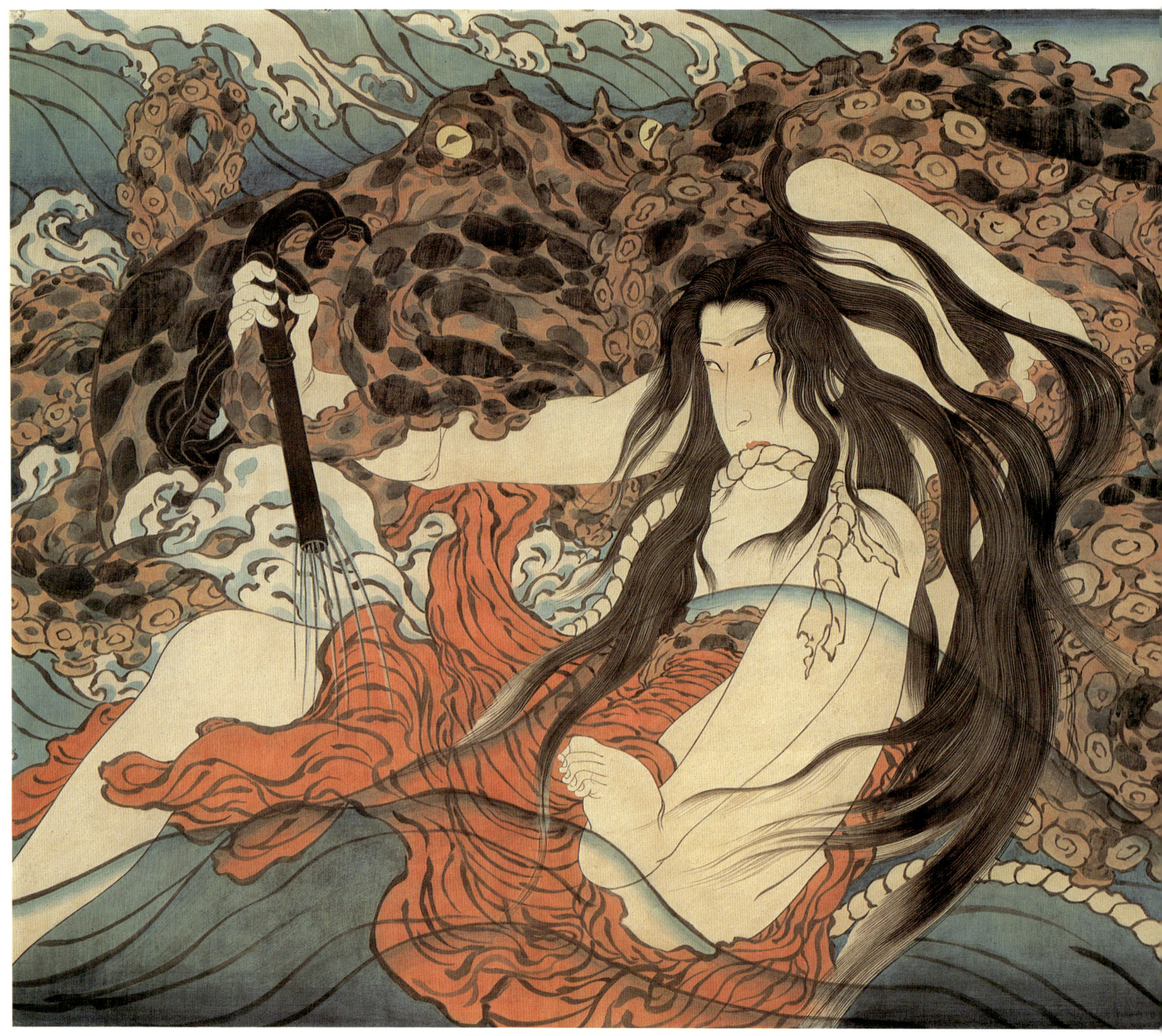

9

WAVE SERIES

PEARL DIVER AND OCTOPUS

1986, watercolor on paper, 32 1/2 × 80 in.
Space Gallery, Los Angeles

The title of this painting, borrowed from Kitagawa Utamaro's (1753–1806) famous *Pearl Diver* series, reads, "Ama ni Tako" (Pearl Diver and Octopus). *Ama ni* also carries the additional meaning of "cooked sweetly," suggesting that cooked octopus with sugar and shoyu is most delicious. To the side of this title, in phonetic kana, is the date equivalent of 1986 and the name of the artist.

The scene pictures a pearl diver (traditionally a woman) writhing to the ocean's surface, entangled in the tentacles of a monstrous octopus, which Teraoka has based on a depiction by Kunisada. The sexual overtone is less explicit than in other works from this series. The finger-like foam of the high waves repeats the shape of the tentacles of the octopus. Its head can barely

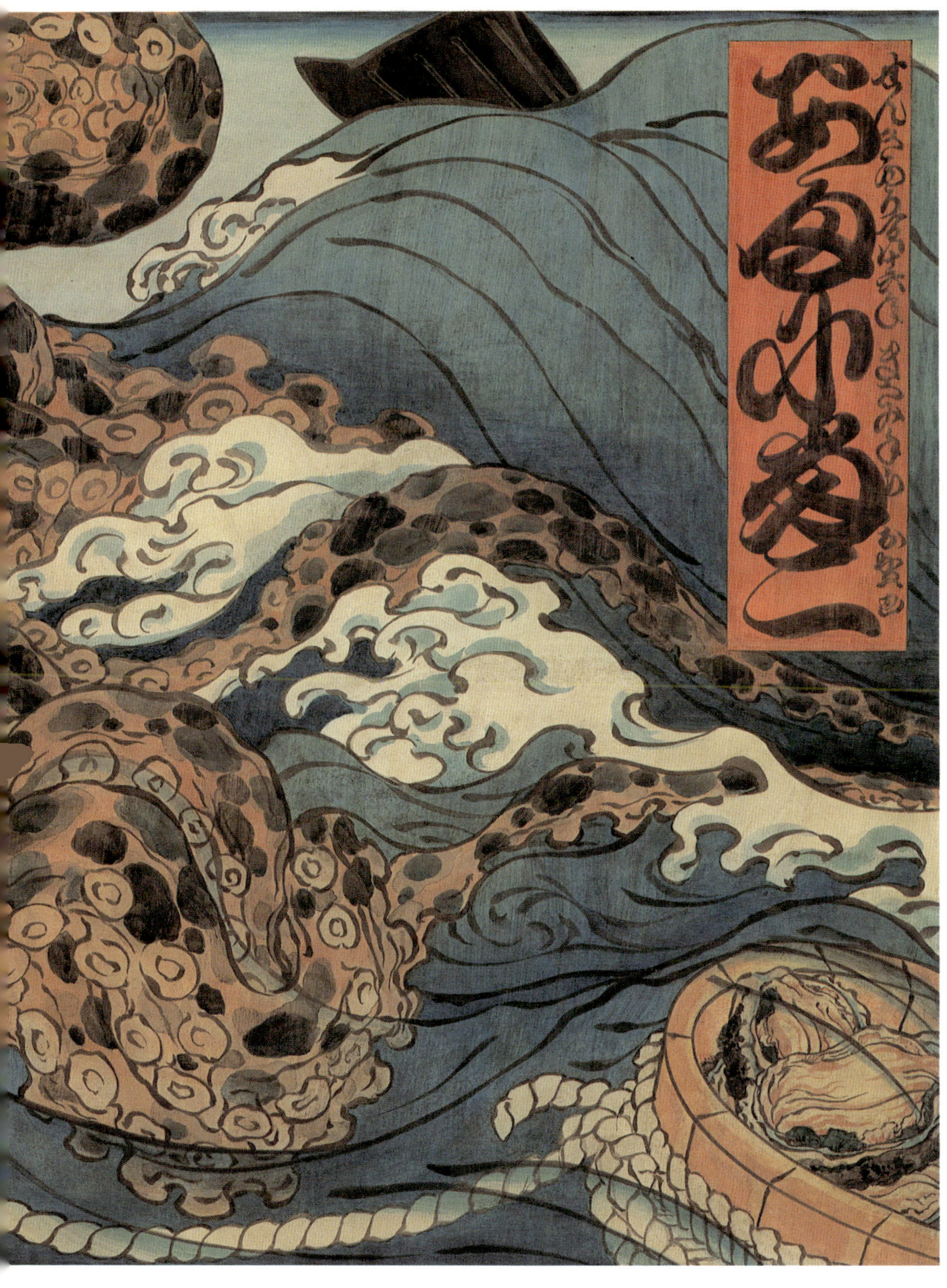

be discerned in the camouflage of its shedding skin; only a beady eye surrounded by a white circular area allows the viewer to identify the form. The Kunisada-like pearl diver, wet black hair cascading down to her buttocks, has removed her water-filled snorkel and has lost one of her fins, which can be seen on the crest of a wave to the right. Attached to a rope held between her teeth is a wooden bucket filled with abalone, a traditional quarry of the pearl diver.

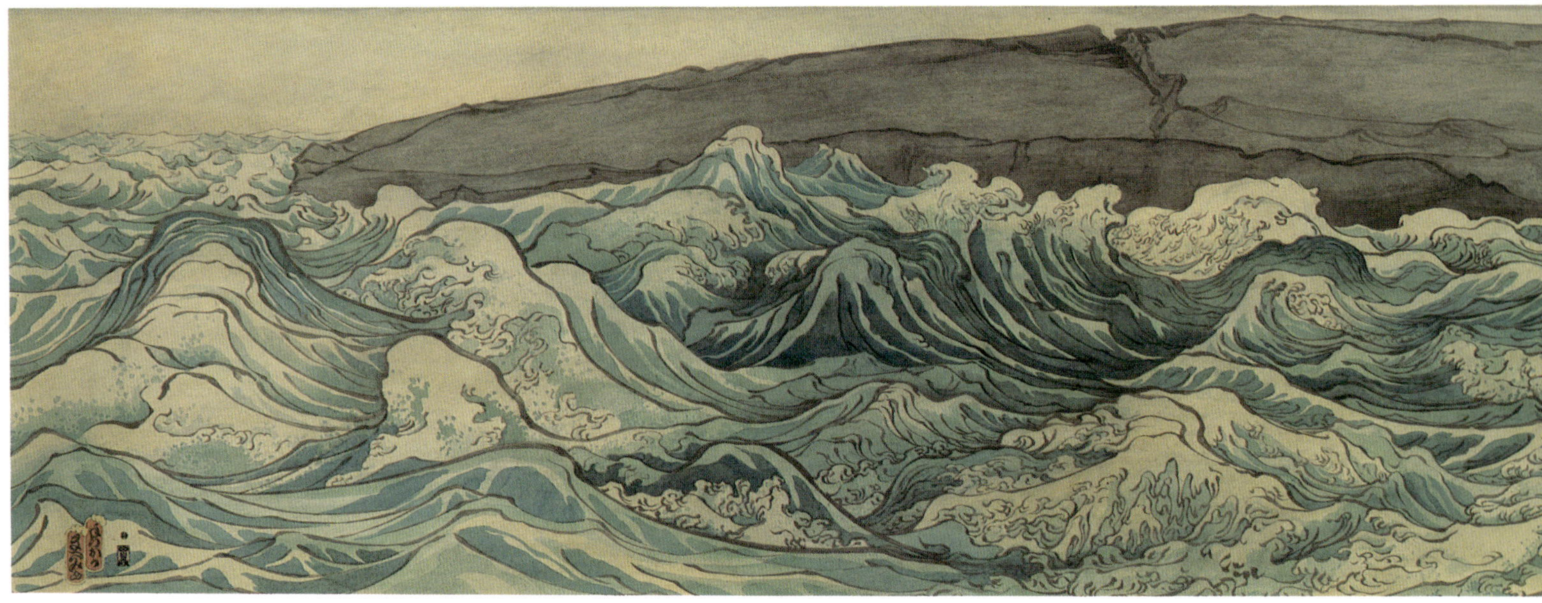

10

WAVE SERIES
TURTLE ISLAND

1984–86, watercolor on paper, mounted as a two-panel screen, 30 × 156 in. Collection of Brad and Penelope Broffman, Los Angeles

In this painting, the latest from the *Wave* series, Teraoka eliminated narrative and erotic elements and focused on nature itself. Gone are the sensuous figures based on Kunisada or Hokusai; instead one sees the churning sea and, rising above the horizon, an impressive island. Viewing the island as sculpture, Teraoka saw in the scene something of the traditional Zen stone gardens of Kyoto and sought to combine the meditative tranquility of Zen with Hawaii's natural beauty.

The composition is in the long handscroll (*emakimono*) format, which is read from right to left. There is something musical about the effect of the painting as one moves visually through the risings and fallings, the climaxes and rest spots, of the composition. This painting paved the way for an unprecedented series dealing with nature.

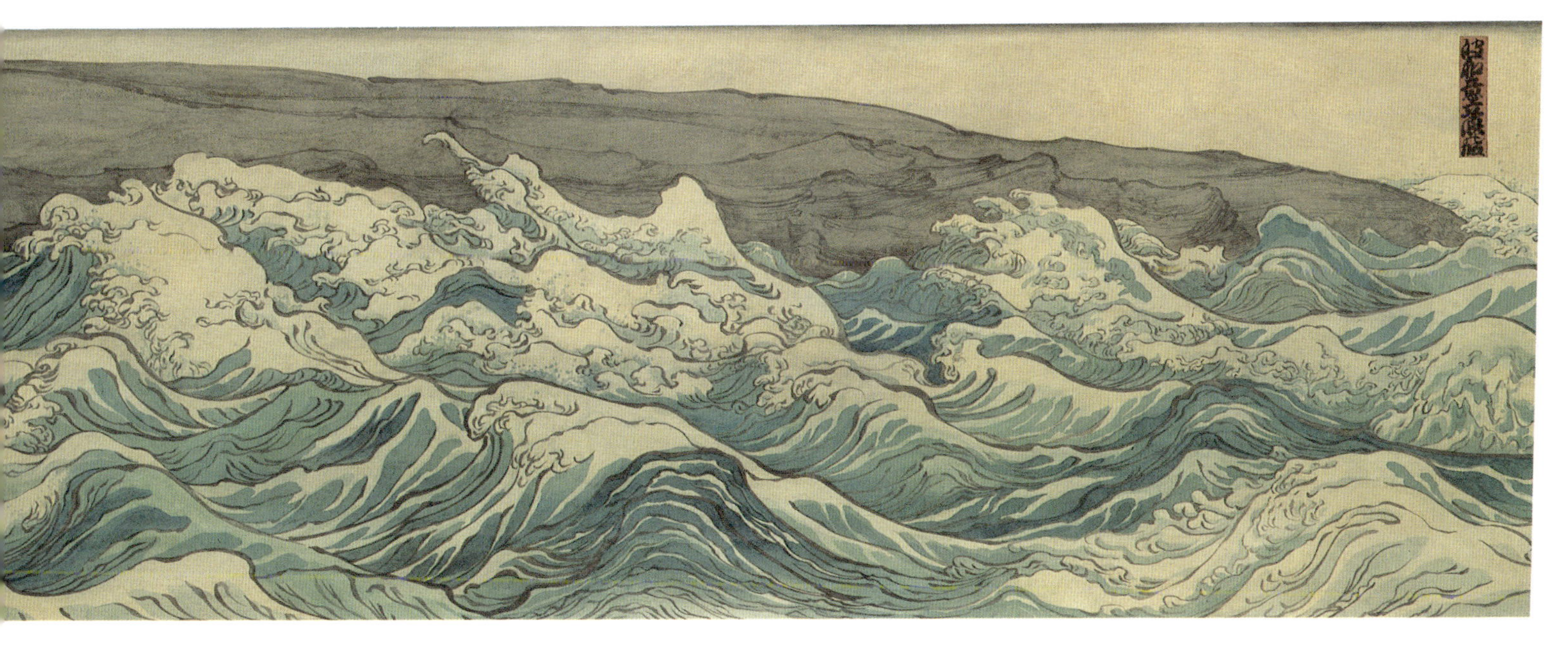

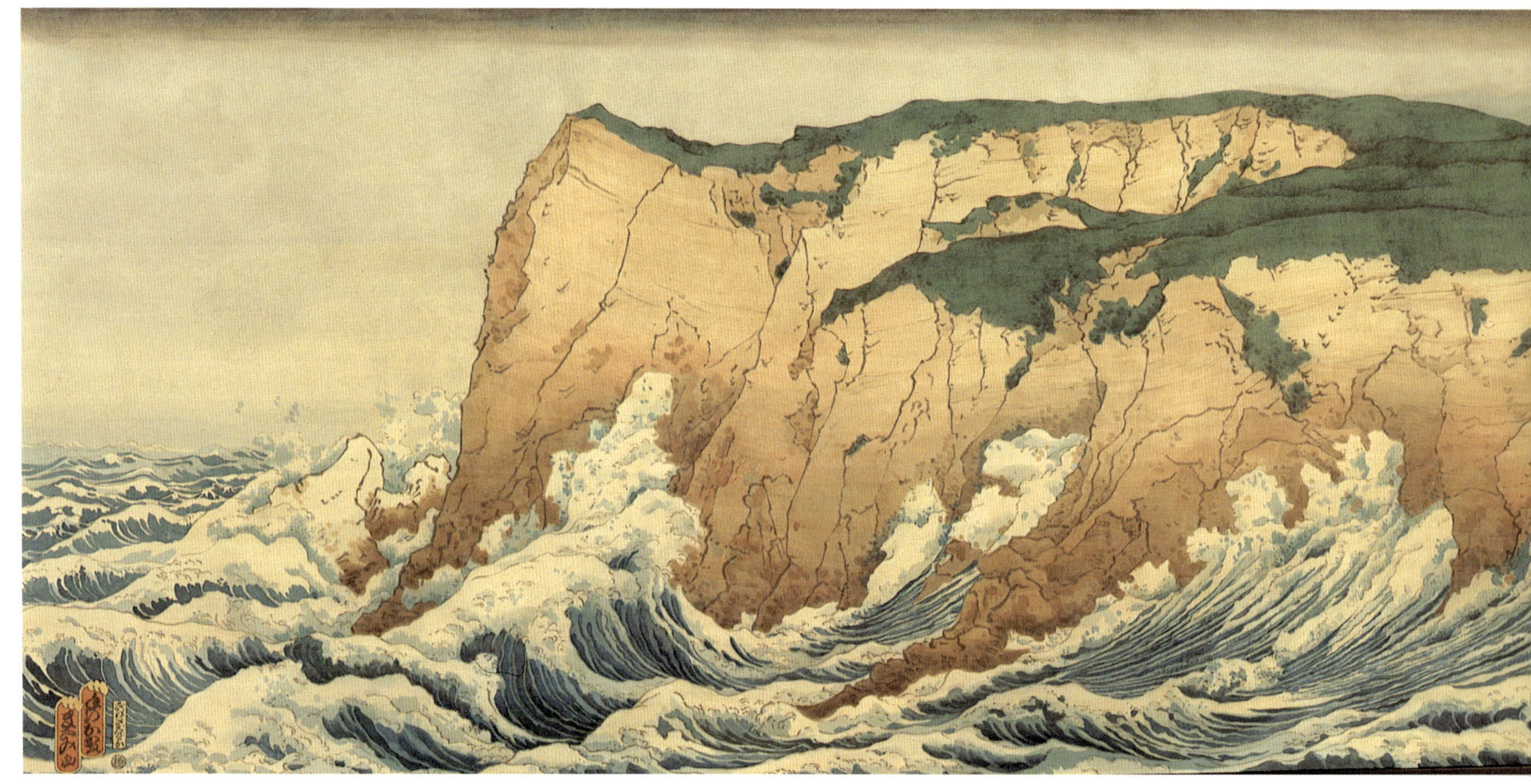

11

CLIFFS AND WAVES

1986–88, watercolor on paper, mounted as a two-panel screen, 38 3/4 × 155 1/2 in.
Space Gallery, Los Angeles

This impressive painting depicting the California coastline and ocean was inspired by Teraoka's visit to Santa Cruz in 1986. The vertical *tanzaku* cartouche on the right identifies the location and indicates that the painting was begun in 1986, when the artist was fifty years old, but not completed until 1988. In truth, the coastline is that of California, but the ocean and its spectacular waves, Teraoka admits, belong to Hawaii. This important work documents Hawaii's impact on Teraoka and his growing obsession with water, whether it be an ocean, a pool, or a waterfall.

In some ways this painting is more Japanese than earlier works by the artist. The cliff, for example, was rendered with the distinctive calligraphic accents of a traditional Japanese brush. Much of the water was done in the same manner, leaving only details to be filled in with a Western brush. That Teraoka should choose to mount the painting in a traditional folding screen (*byōbu*) format is not surprising in light of his use of traditional materials. Along with his own signatures in the Kunisada-like cartouches, he includes the name of the screen maker Sawada Shigeo.

Although the results definitely owe a debt to Hokusai and the cartouches are a reminder of the ukiyo-e print, the brush line is far more vital than the graphic quality of the technical pen used by Teraoka in the 1970s to imitate the woodblock line. Teraoka has here become more painterly, drawing on the traditions of both calligraphic painting and the woodblock. As Teraoka himself suggests, "I've attempted to retain the exaggeration of the woodblock line and surface, but have added painterly elements to see how far I can take it and still have it work." This is one step farther than his usual attempts to replicate the uneven shades of the woodblock print.

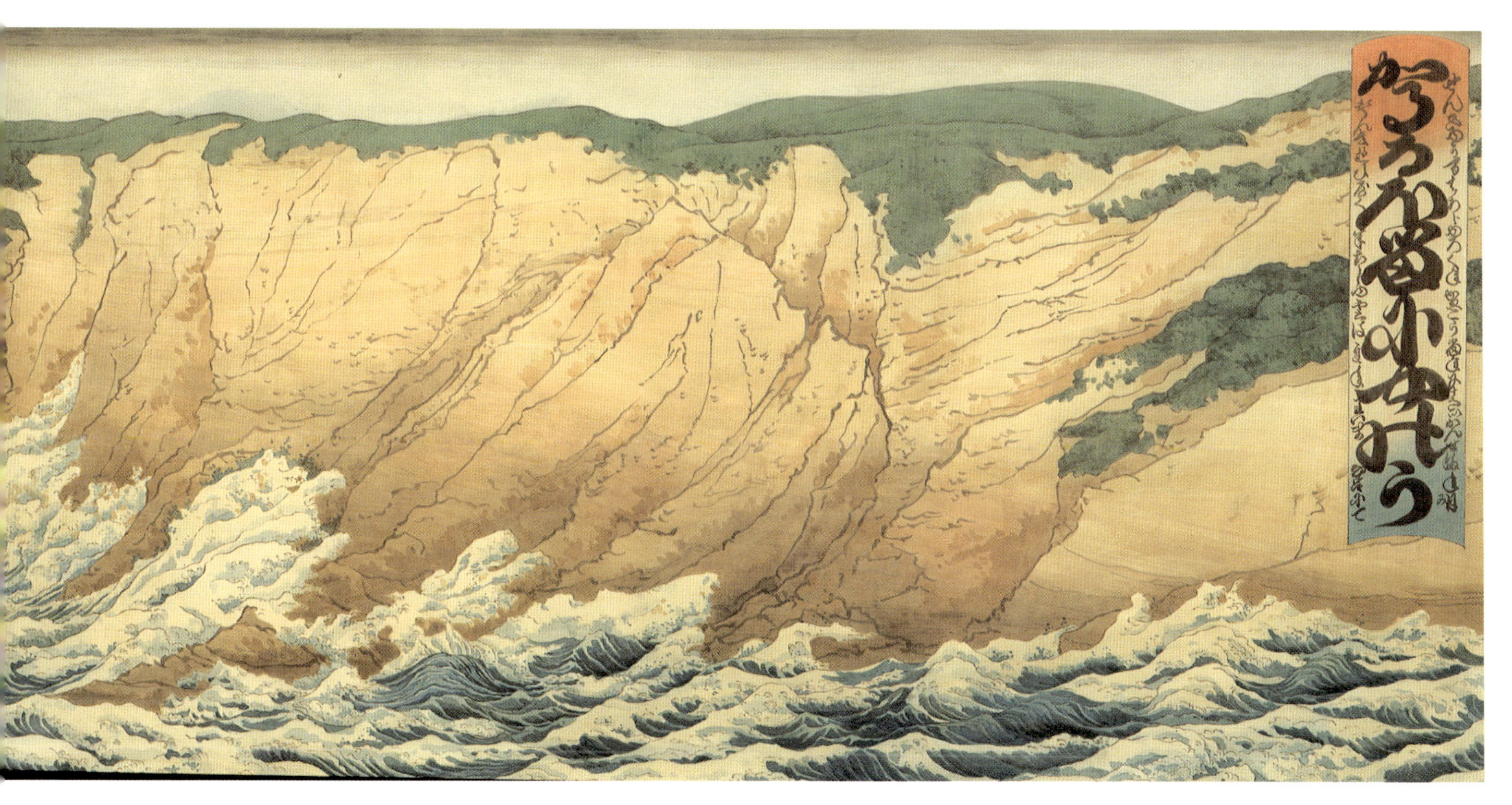

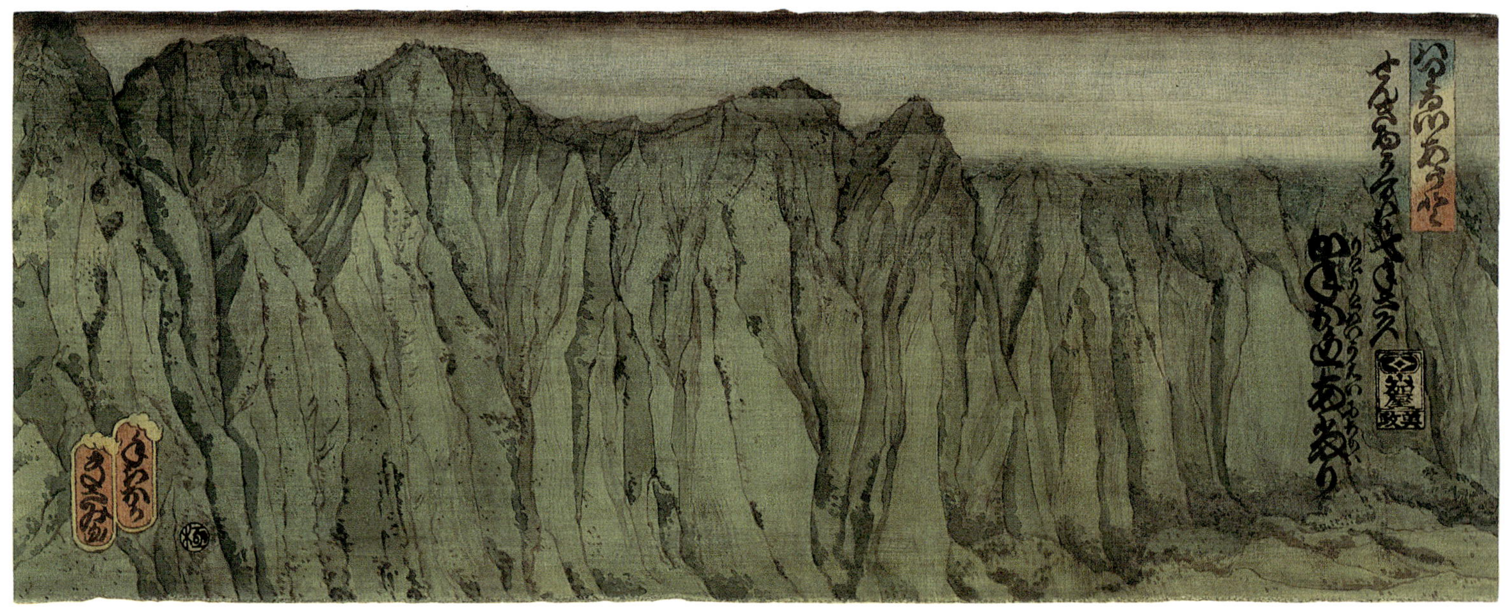

12

PALI LOOKOUT

1987, watercolor on paper, 7 1/2 × 18 1/2 in.
Collection of Edward Den Lau

This small, delicate painting, done in subtle shades of green, features the folds and crevices of the Koolau mountains as viewed from Hawaii's Pali Lookout. Teraoka has delighted in catching the sunlight as it was reflected off the green moss surface of this magnificent mountain range. The effect is very painterly yet totally in keeping with the ukiyo-e print tradition. In fact, Teraoka took great pains to duplicate the actual woodgrain pattern of a landscape print. Calligraphic accents are minimal, and the linear quality is graded—a reminder of Teraoka's debt to ukiyo-e. He also included a multi-colored cartouche, at the far right, reading "Pali Lookout" and the year, 1987. In the left corner, Kunisada-like red cartouches read "Masami" and "Teraoka," and the ever-present censorship seal reads "kiwame."

This painting shows a direct relationship to the work of Teraoka's relative, the artist Chikkyō Ono (b. 1889), and the painting tradition he fostered. This Japanese-style painter, born in Okayama and a graduate of the Kyoto College of Fine Arts, influenced Teraoka in his earlier career as a landscape artist. *Pali Lookout* shows the typical blending of Japanese-style painting and European influence, the essential qualities of which are a graphic flatness combined with Western values of light and shade. The result is a subtly decorative coloration of great beauty.

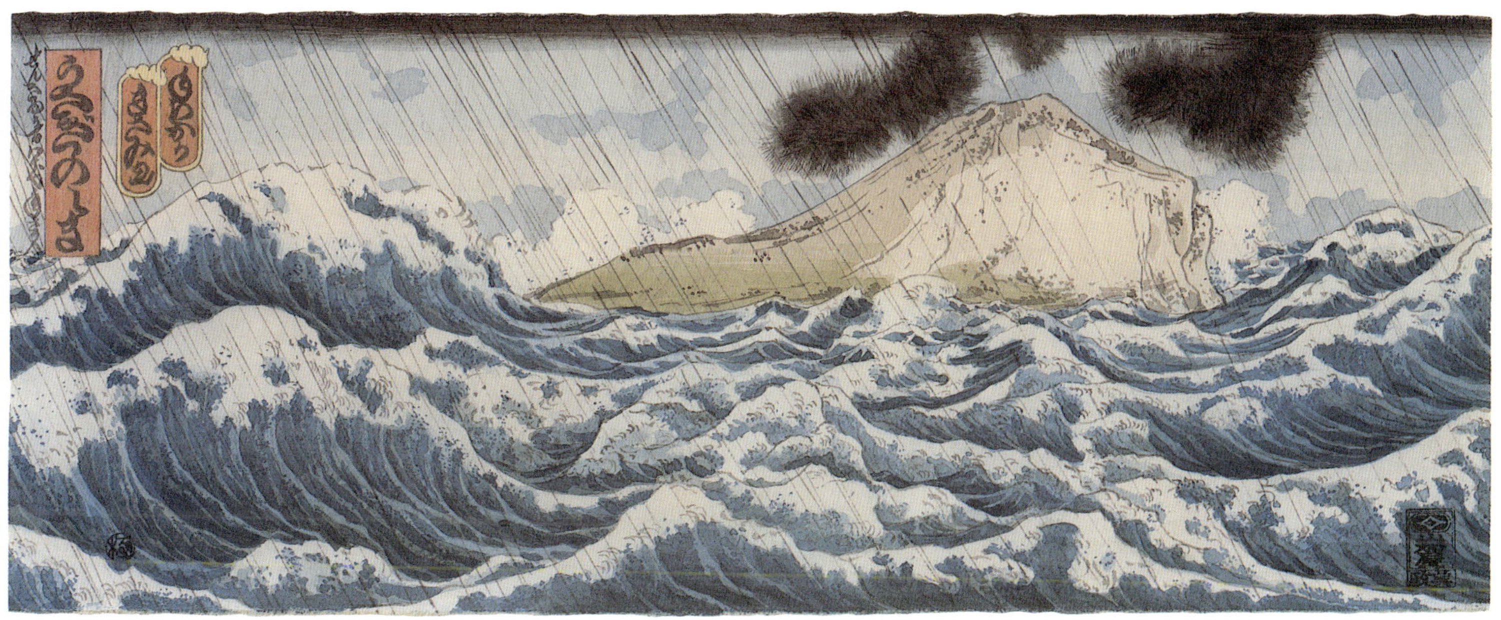

13

WET RABBIT ISLAND

1987, watercolor on paper, 7 1/2 × 18 1/2 in.
Private collection

Like Pali Lookout, Rabbit Island is a landmark unique to Hawaii. Teraoka painted a picturesque scene of the island in 1987, drawing on the art of Hokusai and of one of Hokusai's followers, Yashima Gakutei (c. 1786–1868). (The same influences can be seen in *Makapuu Beach* (cat. no. 14) and *Molokai Lookout Point*.) Evidence of Gakutei's influence in *Wet Rabbit Island* is apparent in the depiction of the churning waves and in the introduction of storm clouds that descend from heaven as if they were black smoke. The large red *tanzaku* cartouche on the far left reads "Rabbit Island" and a long inscription outside the cartouche dates the work to 1987. Two additional cartouches read "Masami" and "Teraoka." As in most of Teraoka's landscape compositions, the setting is devoid of human narrative.

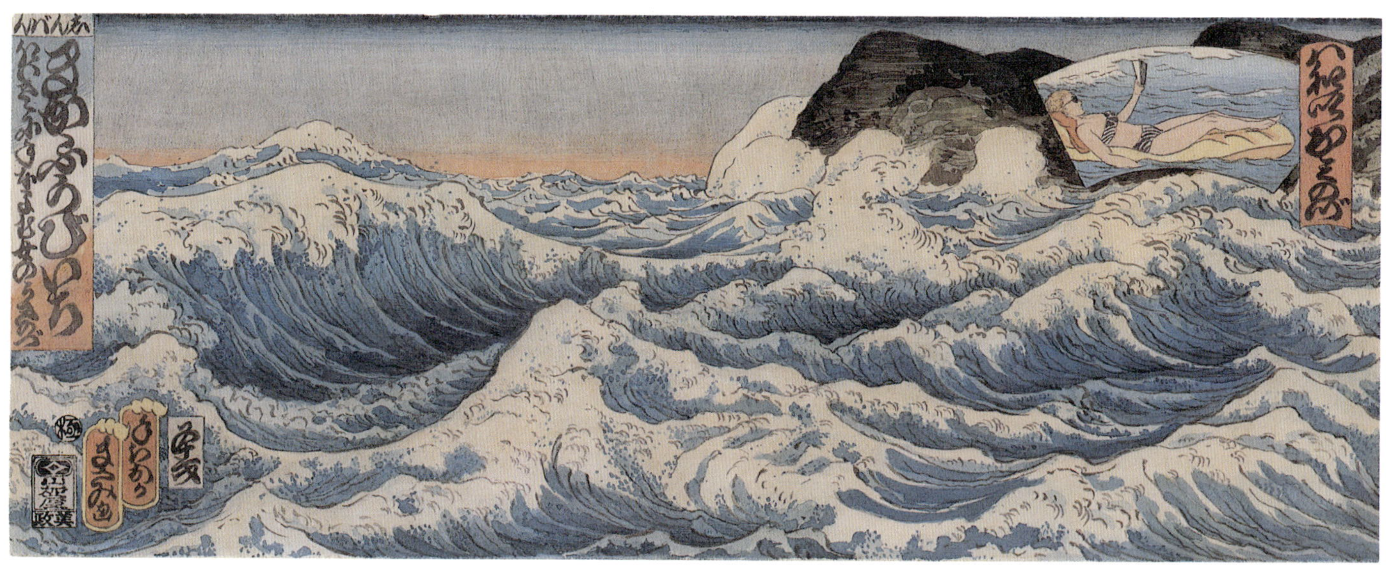

14

MAKAPUU BEACH

1987, watercolor on paper, 7 3/8 × 18 1/2 in.
Private collection

The influence of Gakutei can also be seen in this superb small painting featuring a storm at Makapuu Beach. The composition was rendered with a Western brush for its small line; only the large calligraphic lines were done with a traditional Japanese brush. The red cartouche to the right translates, "Painting of Waves"; the fan-shaped insert shows a blonde Caucasian woman (Teraoka's model was Lynda Hess) reading a book on an inflatable float at Waikiki Beach. Teraoka intended to contrast the two sides of Oahu Island: the rough turbulence of the shore at Makapuu and the calm ocean of Waikiki Beach.

The usual signature seals, reading "Masami" and "Teraoka," are included along with the family crest of his family's kimono shop, presented as if it were a publisher's seal. A censorship (*kiwame*) seal completes the deception. Other inscriptions suggest that Masami was fifty years old at the time of this painting; he was actually one year older.

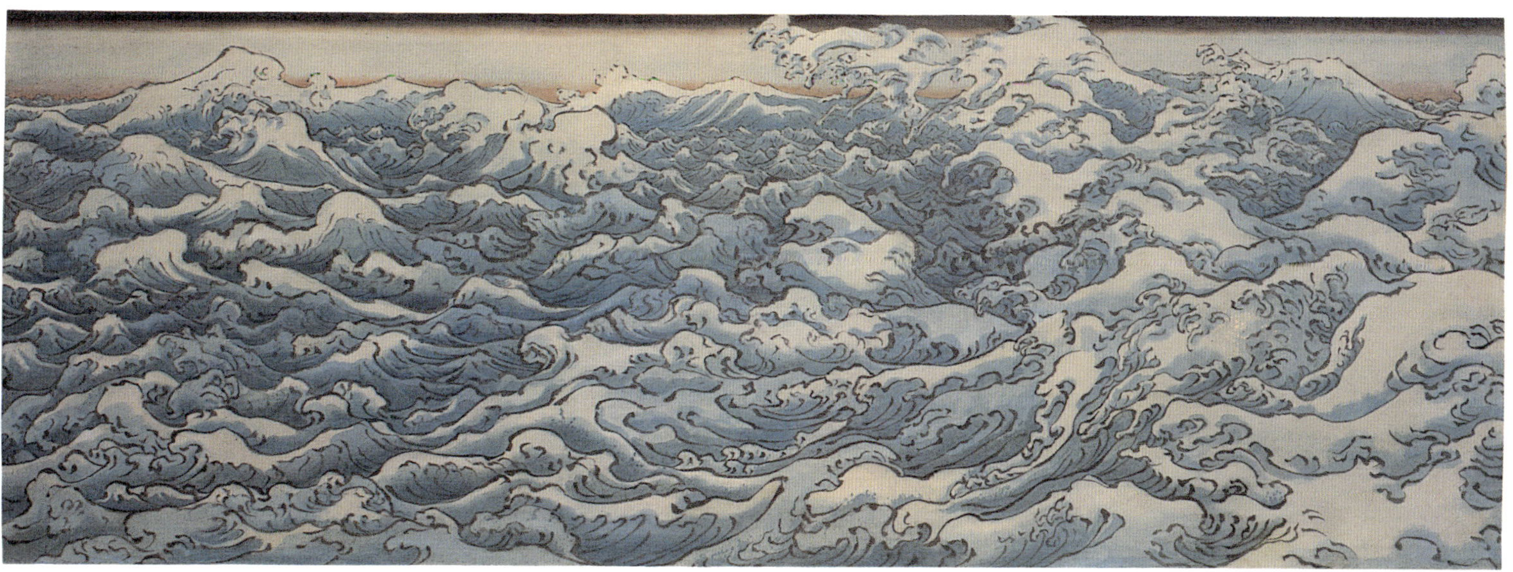

15

WAVES

1986, watercolor on canvas, mounted as a horizontal scroll, 53 1/2 × 184 3/4 in. Space Gallery, Los Angeles

This splendid painting of waves is mounted as a long horizontal scroll. Although the format is not ideal for display on a wall, the use of a roller makes it easy to store the work and serves as a subtle reminder that the painting was derived from the "time art" associated with the handscroll.

The churning ocean and its whitecaps are magnificently rendered. The painting is devoid of figures, and not even a cartouche or signature invades the scene. The composition is reminiscent of paintings by artists as far back as the Muromachi period (1392–1568), but a more direct comparison might be found in the wave paintings of Rimpa school artists such as Sakai Hōitsu (1761–1828) and Suzuki Kiitsu (1796–1858). *The Great Wave* from Hokusai's famed *Mt. Fuji* series was also a source of inspiration for this work.

Teraoka began the painting in New York City at the Soho studio of a friend, from whom he borrowed this large canvas intended for oils or acrylics. The artist sized the canvas with alum and rabbit-skin glues, which are usually used to size paper to prepare it for watercolor. The spectacular results seem closer to the tradition of ink painting than to the hard-lined results of the woodblock print. The only reminder of Teraoka's debt to the woodblock medium is the dark skyline at the top edge of the painting, a convention borrowed from the landscape prints of both Hokusai and Hiroshige.

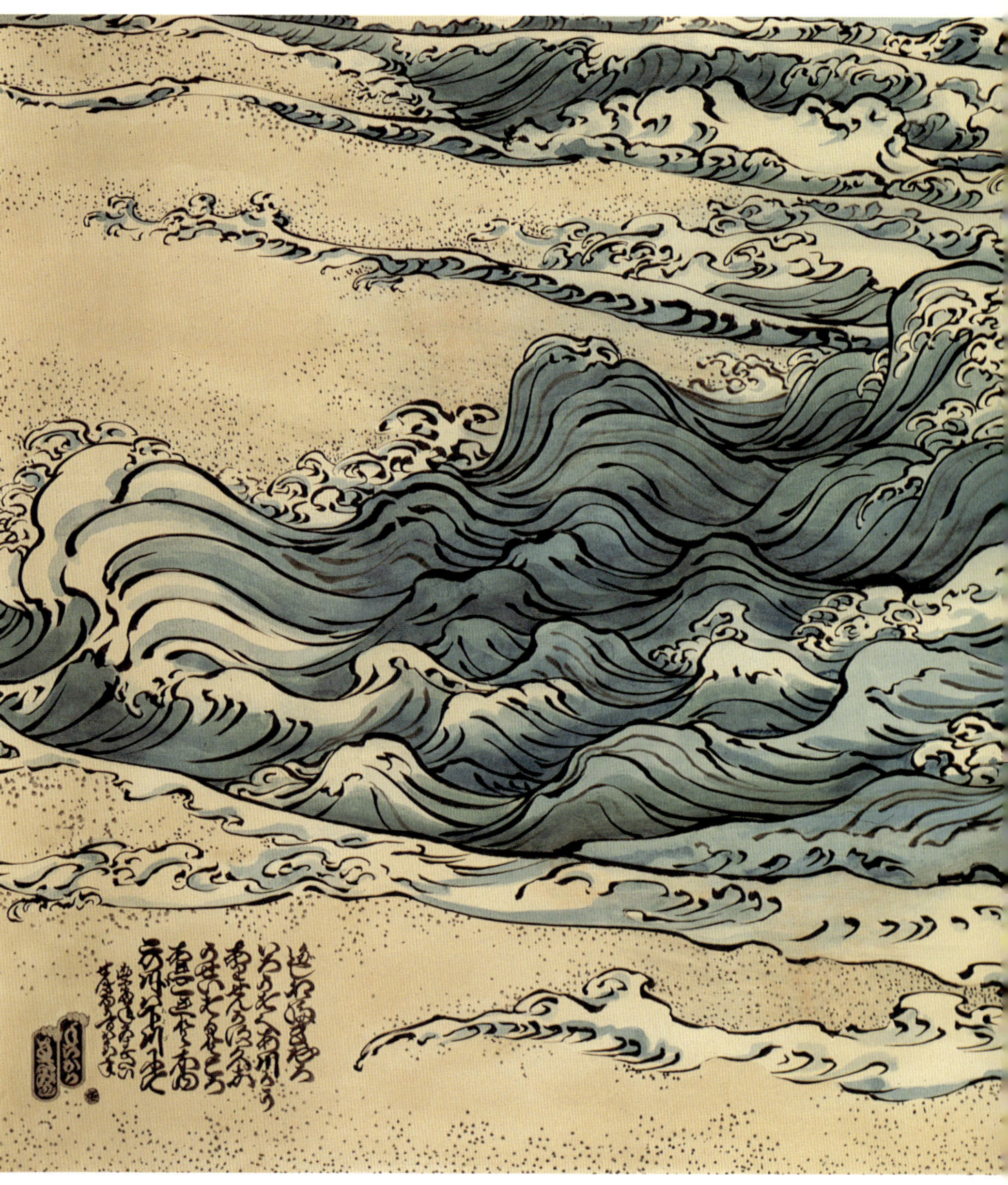

16

WAVES: WAIMANALO BEACH

1986–88, watercolor and sumi ink study on paper, mounted as a scroll, 42 × 94 in. Space Gallery, Los Angeles

In comparison with *Pali Lookout* (cat. no. 12) or *Cliffs and Waves* (cat. no. 11), both of which show combined Japanese and Western influences, this superb large painting of whitecaps moving toward a stippled shoreline (reminiscent of Japanese sprinkled gold flecks) is purely Japanese in feeling and execution. Inspired by the great waves of Waimanalo Beach, where Teraoka's studio is located, the painting describes the great waves and their turbulence in dynamic terms.

The work presages Teraoka's growing interest in traditional Japanese techniques and has a special freshness that is completely different from earlier works: the painting's transparency of color and vitality and spontaneity of line are immediately appealing. This is the first painting in which Teraoka introduced sumi ink for the black line, and he used a Japanese brush for the entire painting. The results are truly outstanding, and this writer suspects that in the future the subtle warmth and immediacy of sumi ink will play an increasingly important role in Teraoka's work.

Teraoka painted directly on the huge paper without a preconceived composition. The ocean and its waves virtually dance across the space; the

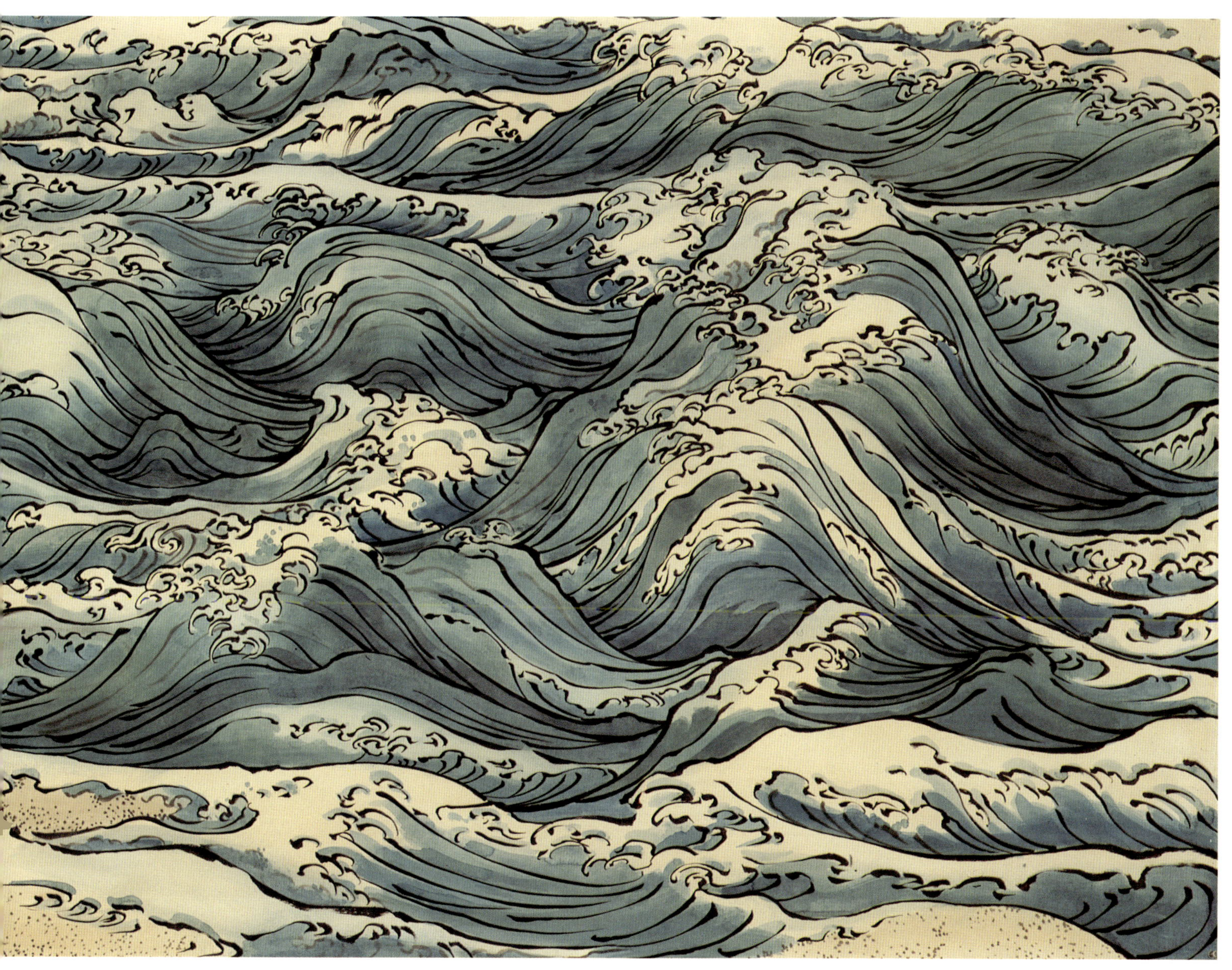

fingers of the ocean crawl up the sandy beach without mind or purpose. The painting reveals Teraoka's abilities as both painter and draftsman; one can see hints of the great ink tradition of Japan's Muromachi period. Admittedly the work is a study, and Teraoka himself complains about the uneven tonal values of some of the blacks. For example, in the left-hand corner, next to the two Kunisada-like cartouches bearing the names "Masami" and "Teraoka," is an inscription announcing that this is a "sudden painting" and that many places are to be redone. Because of the nature of the space, the inscription reads from left to right rather than the traditional right to left. The commentary also indicates that some lines and colors should be lighter. All of this suggests that Teraoka has recognized the potential of sumi ink in terms of its cool and warm shadings. Like *Waves* (cat. no. 15), this work was begun in 1986 in New York City but was not completed until 1988 at Teraoka's Waimanalo studio.

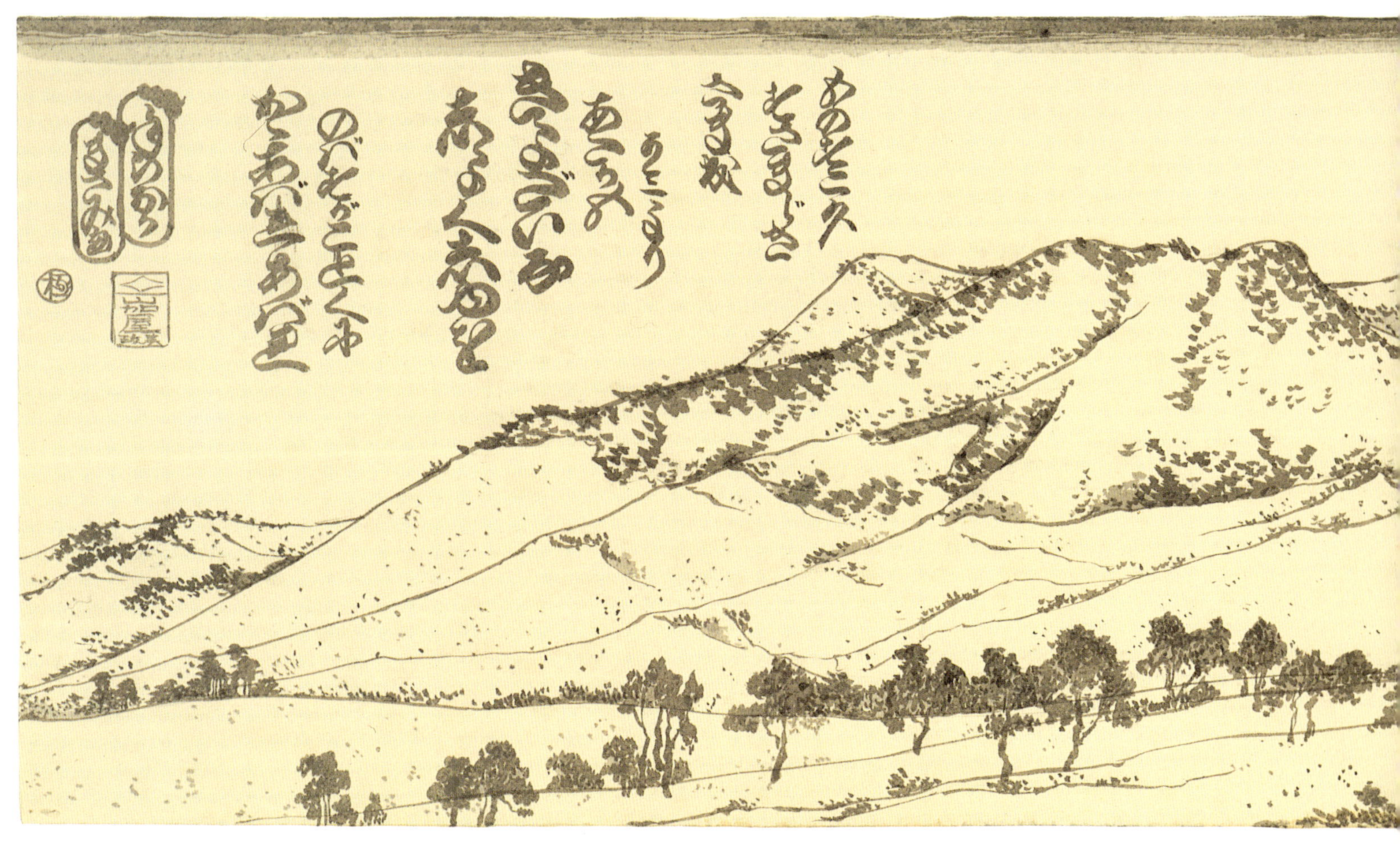

17

NEW VIEWS OF KOKO HEAD

1987, watercolor study on paper, 10 1/2 × 37 in.
Collection of the artist

This black and white watercolor done with a Japanese brush owes a great debt to the painting style of Teraoka's relative, Chikkyō Ono. As in the last example (cat. no. 16), no preparatory drawings were made for this work; the artist painted the scene from memory in his studio. The inscription indicates that the scene is a view of Koko Head, a view that changes continually depending on the time of day and the quality of light. On this day it rained, and the waves at nearby Makapuu were particularly high and violent, writhing up like the tentacles of a giant squid. Despite the inscription, the scene is relatively calm and does not document the Makapuu waves. The usual signature cartouches, censorship seal, and kimono shop crest are inscribed to the left.

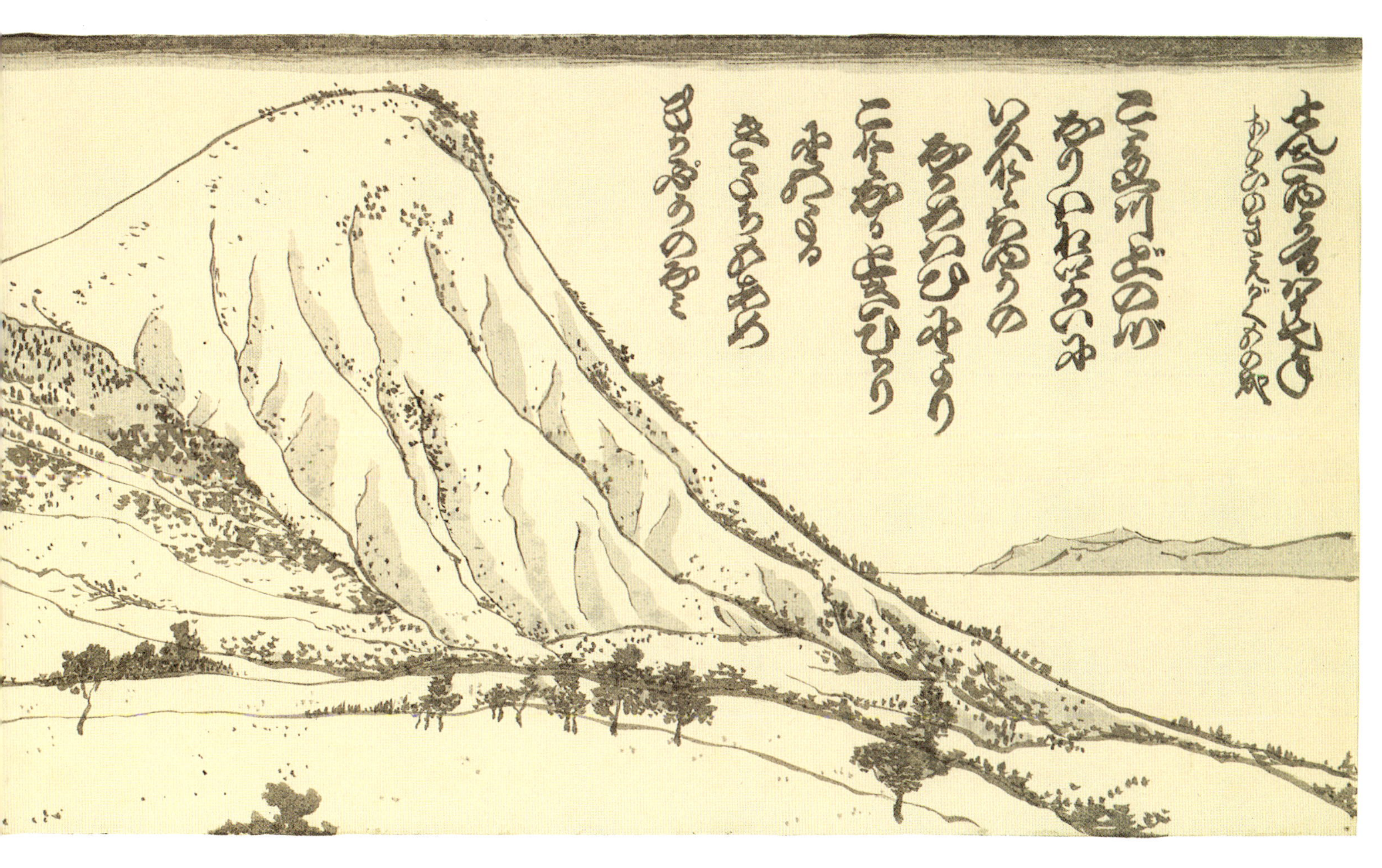

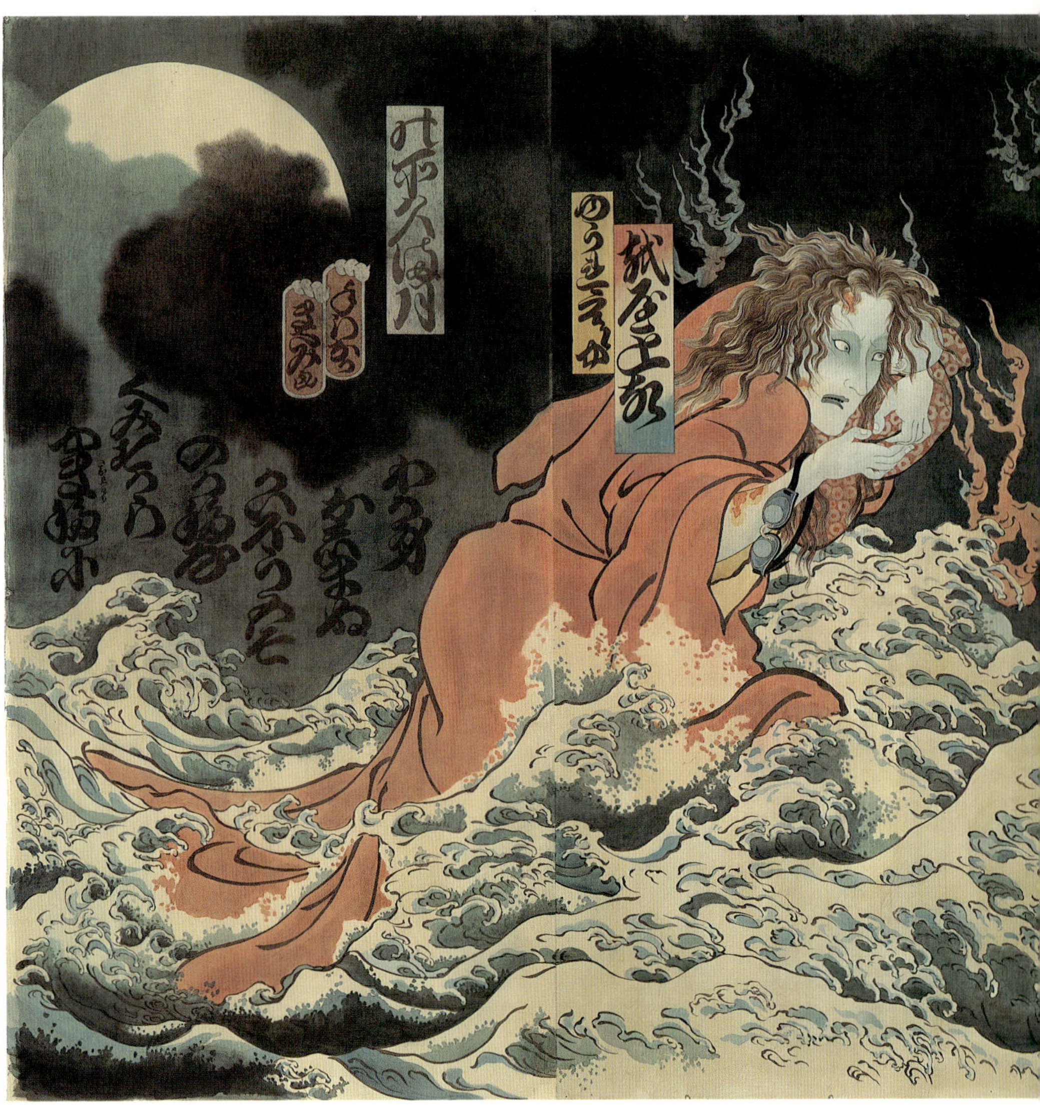

18

AMERICAN KABUKI: OISHIIWA

1986, watercolor on paper, mounted as a four-panel screen, 77 1/2 × 155 in. Space Gallery, Los Angeles

This four-panel screen conveys the shock and grief that Teraoka felt on learning that a friend's newborn child had contracted Acquired Immune Deficiency Syndrome (AIDS) as the result of a contaminated blood transfusion. The scene is done in the manner of a kabuki stage performance with a number of symbolic allusions unique to that theater.

The word *oishii* in the title means delicious; *wa* is added as a kind of feminine emphasis. This play on words refers to Oiwa, Japan's most feared ghost, who is almost always depicted with an ugly, bulging bruise on one eye. Oiwa was a famous heroine of the kabuki ghost tale *Yotsuya Kaidan*: cruelly murdered by her husband, she came back from the grave to wreak bloody vengeance. In Teraoka's expressively bizarre and startling screen, we see the metamorphosed visages of mother and child smoldering in the flames of other ghostly souls (other AIDS victims), who rise from a churning sea to avenge the injustice of it all. What did Teraoka intend by changing the title from "Oiwa" to "Oishiiwa," meaning "very delicious?" Does he refer to the ghost's victims? Or is he making reference to the declamation of a woman who is enjoying the act of love making? Both messages work profoundly well within the scope of Teraoka's imagery, but surely the primary message to all is that delicious love making should be cautiously pursued, for everyone is at risk.

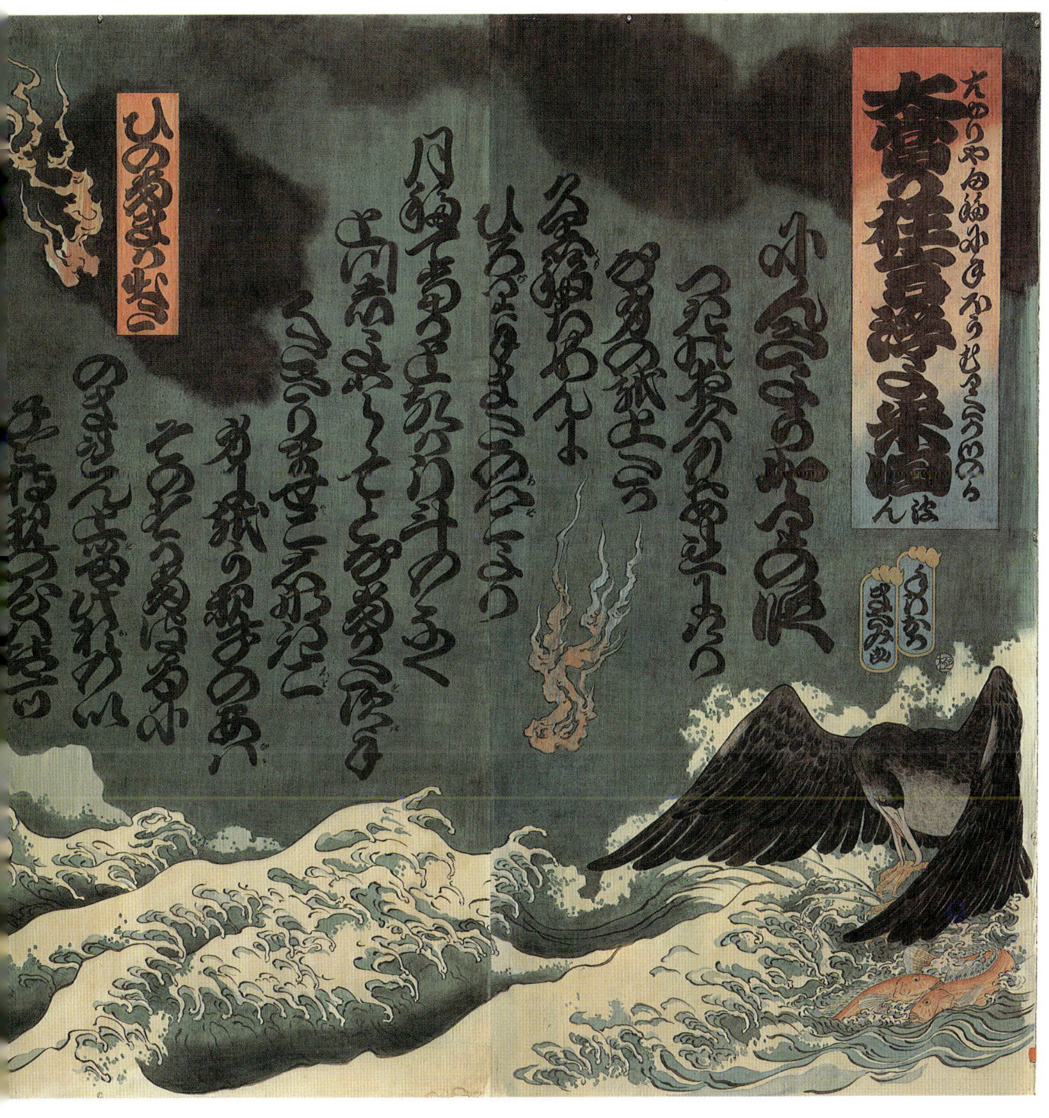

To the right of the ghostly vision is a frigate bird with long powerful wings. These birds are known to steal fish out of the mouths of other diving birds, and perhaps Teraoka was symbolizing the virus itself, for it too steals life. The moon in the left panel symbolizes hope, according to Teraoka, and the continuity of life, but it is being suffocated by dark black clouds, which occur throughout the screen. These clouds suggest fear and death. The calligraphy that moves across the painting is a narrative: "In the evening, clouds are very turbulent, storm bearing. The sound of the waves is loud, and black clouds are beginning to spread over the shoreline. As the evening wears on, the full moon is revealed when the clouds part. Suddenly a cry is heard: 'Help us! Help us!' But it is so faint that the audience is uncertain as to whether they heard a voice or if it is only the sound of the waves."

This was the first in a series of paintings focusing on the subject of AIDS. In subsequent paintings Teraoka utilized the symbolism of the kabuki stage to extend his message on all aspects of the dread disease. That Teraoka should choose to parody the Oiwa theme is in keeping with his great love of Kunisada and Hokusai, both of whom produced prints on the subject of *Yotsuya Kaidan*.

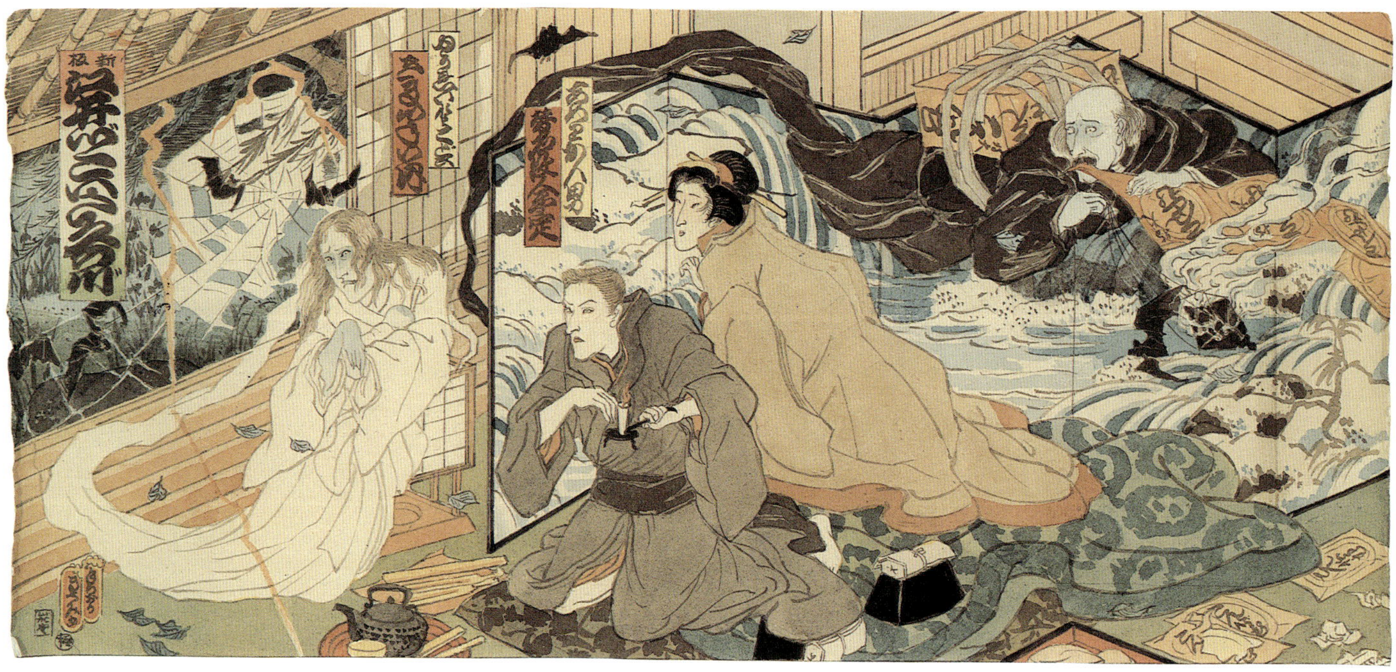

19

AIDS SERIES GHOST OF KYOTO INN

1987, watercolor study on paper,
$10\,^{1}/_{2} \times 22\,^{1}/_{2}$ in.
Space Gallery, Los Angeles

In this splendid watercolor study Teraoka has created a kabuki-like scene in which a ghost appears in the private quarters of an American who has been engaged in sex with a courtesan. The American holds a candle in one hand; the expression on his face is cautious, even apprehensive. The courtesan seems to listen for some sound beyond the folding screen. She feels and hears a strange wind: *"doro, doro."* She sees the ghost of a woman with her baby, the same ghost, perhaps, as the one in Teraoka's first major AIDS painting, *American Kabuki/Oishiiwa* (cat. no. 18). Above, drifting over the folding screen, is the ghost of a Catholic priest with a box of condoms strapped to his back. With one hand and his teeth he attempts to open a condom wrapper; the other hand precariously grasps a censer used in High Mass. The scene is reminiscent of the ghost stories of Lafcadio Hearn; bats and spiderwebs add to the effect.

As in all of Teraoka's narrative compositions, little is left unexplained. The large cartouche to the left indicates that this is a new woodblock-style series dealing with tactics against the disease AIDS. The mercurial ghost and baby are identified in cartouche, although curiously the name of the kabuki actor who will play the role has yet to be decided. The same is true of the American; the actor's name is omitted. Perhaps Teraoka is saying that the actors shun roles related to this dread disease for fear of public ridicule and scandal.

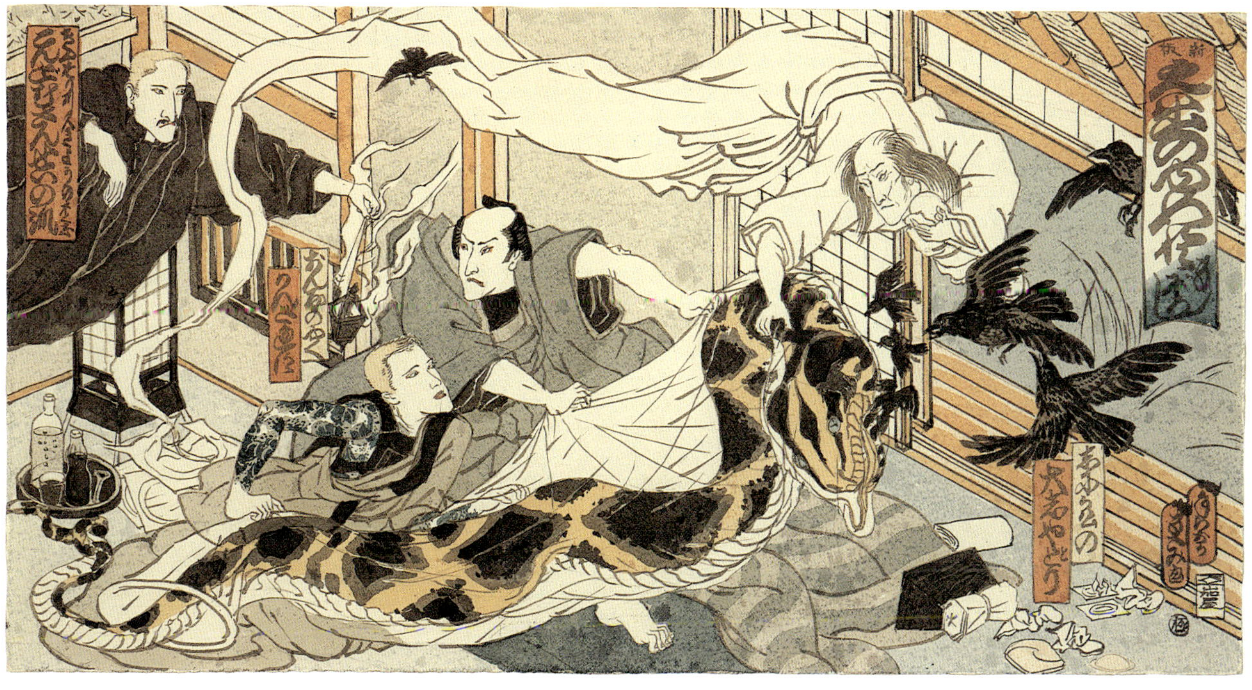

20

AIDS SERIES

KYOTO INN: GHOST AND SNAKE

1987, watercolor study on paper, 10 1/2 × 19 1/2 in.
Space Gallery, Los Angeles

Set in the same Kyoto Inn as the last example (cat. no. 19), this kabuki stage scene depicts a tattooed blonde woman and a samurai who are placing a huge condom over a giant snake, the symbol of AIDS and sex, in an attempt to suffocate it. Blackbirds hover around the snake, screeching and flying about in a threatening manner, while above, the ghost of a man carrying a baby helps the two principals to trap the snake in the condom. Coming through the open veranda is a Catholic priest wearing black robes. He too is a ghost and enters to help teach those who are still living to use the condom for survival.

Again Teraoka has provided ample identifications for the scene. The large multicolored cartouche to the right translates: "The Nightmare of AIDS and the Haunting of Ghosts." Cartouches near the hovering blackbirds (*karasu*) indicate bad luck. Indeed, crows have been regarded as ill omens in Japan from an early date and generally have been regarded as disagreeable birds, universally shooed away from farmers' vegetable patches and looked upon as dour, quarrelsome, and unpoetic creatures. Teraoka here has taken up these uncouth birds, playing with their bold shapes to suggest their evilness and at the same time recalling the Japanese superstition that a crow flying over a house means death within. Still other cartouches indicate that the snake is dying; others identify the Catholic priest and imply that the Catholic Church should condone the condom.

21

AIDS SERIES

GEISHA AND FOX

1988, watercolor on paper, 14 3/4 × 25 in.

Space Gallery, Los Angeles

In kabuki, the fox (*kitsune*) has always been something of a prankster and often appears as a ghost. Borrowing this image, Teraoka here uses the fox as the symbol for AIDS. He is dragging a courtesan down to hell, tearing at her kimono. The courtesan is surrounded by bubbling lava, and the sensual face of the trickster is full of success, for despite the geisha's attempt to protect herself with a condom, it is already too late. Teraoka has not explicitly identified the characters of this close-up narrative. The vertical *tanzaku* cartouche to the far right with a bridge post at the top, signifying perhaps the bridge between earth and hell, has an inscription that translates "Woman, fox, and lava."

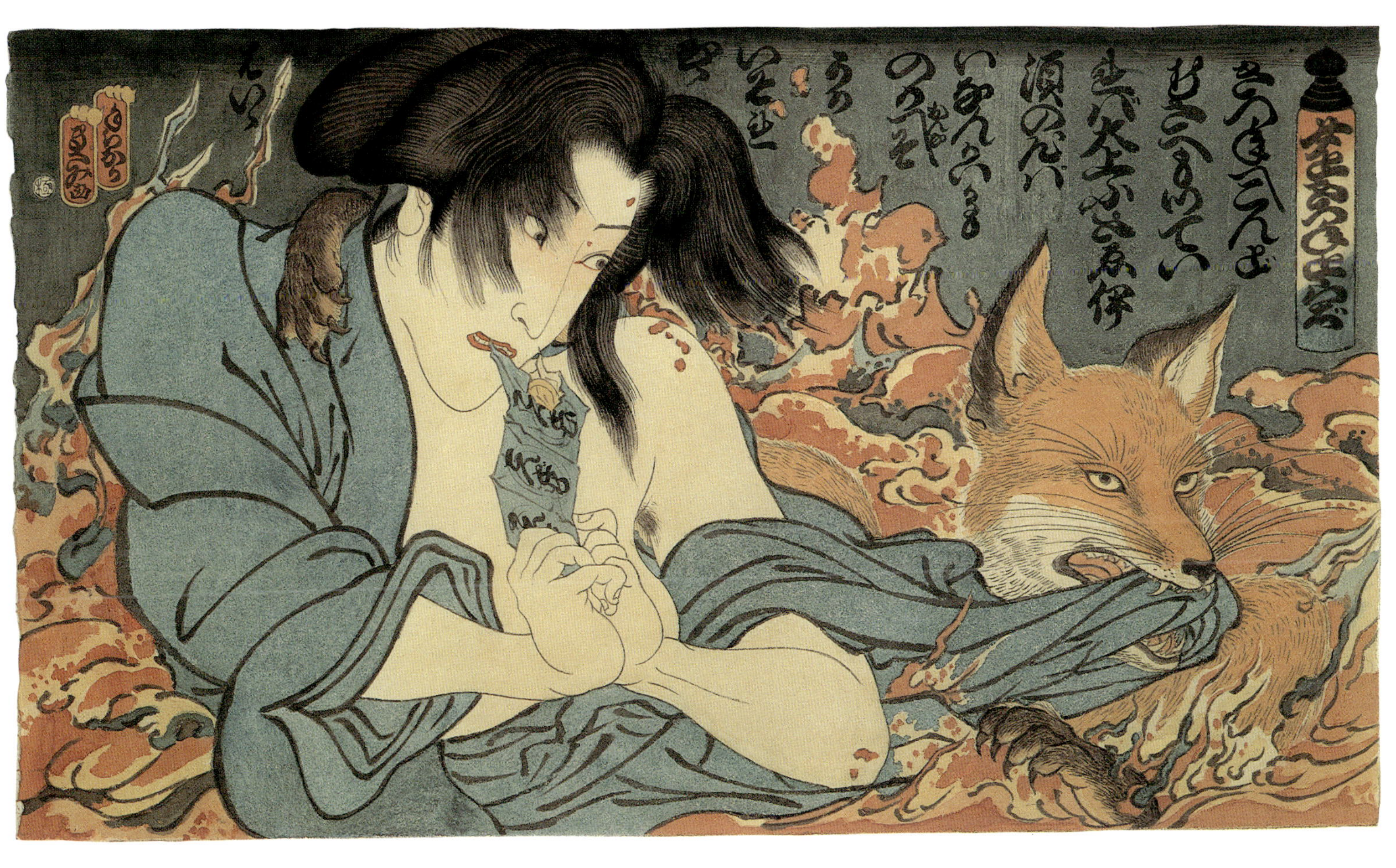

22

AIDS SERIES GEISHA AND SKELETON

1987, watercolor study on paper, 22 1/4 × 15 in.
Space Gallery, Los Angeles

In this vertical composition a courtesan with heavy, exaggerated hairpins and haircombs is seated on the floor beside her warmer (*hibachi*). She attempts to bite open the outer wrappers of two condom packages. Her dead boyfriend opens a window to the room; his hand is that of a skeleton. The scene is shocking in its implications but beautiful in its sheer artistry. The painting bears a date in cartouche in the lower right: "1987, artist at the age of fifty-two years." Two Kunisada-style cartouches identify the artist's name.

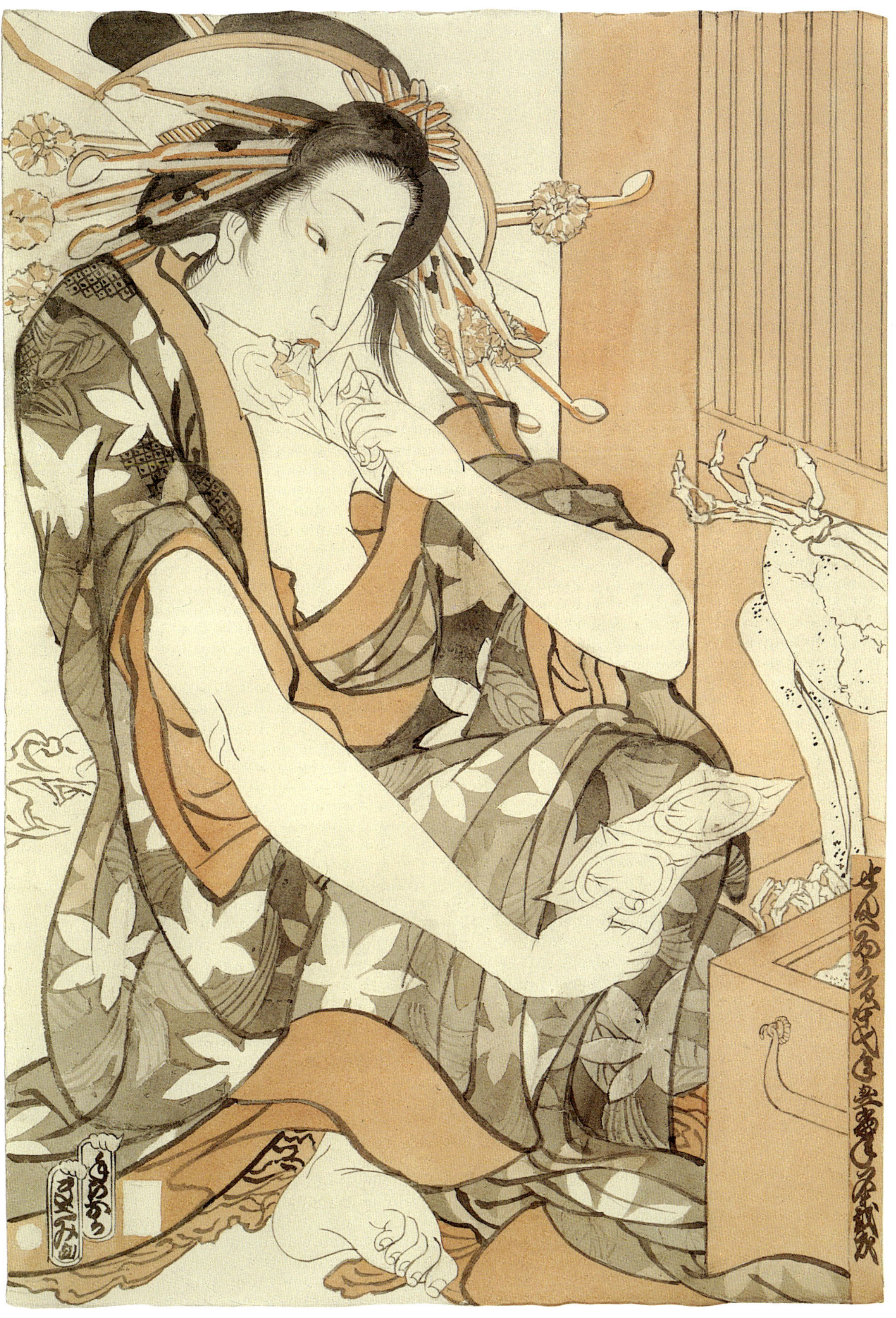

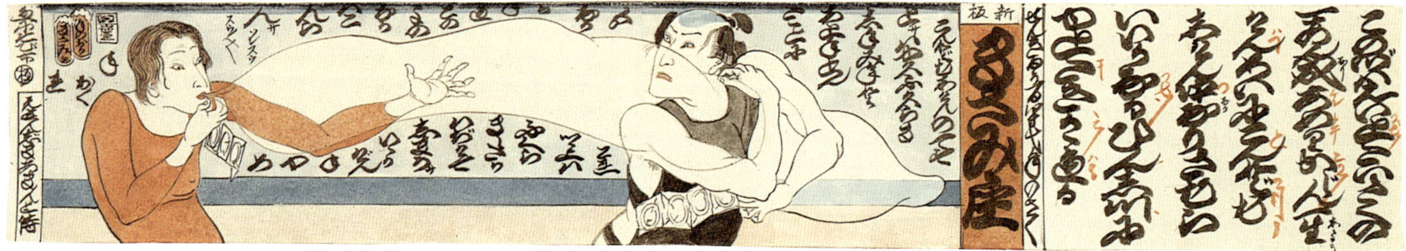

AIDS SERIES SANTA MONICA BEACH

1987, watercolor study on paper, 4 × 22 in.
Space Gallery, Los Angeles

Teraoka placed this AIDS scene at Santa Monica Beach, the setting of some of his earlier paintings. A Caucasian woman with short brown hair and a samurai are testing the strength of a huge condom. The woman's chest has become concave from blowing air into the condom, which the samurai hugs to prevent it from blowing in the wind. The long horizontal composition is reinforced by the elongated condom and the endless beach. The stances of the protagonists have a feeling of imbalance, as if the woman and the samurai were on roller skates, a condition beautifully suggested by Teraoka without being explicit.

The long inscription to the right and continuing behind the figures describes the scene in detail. "This is one of the projects to protect yourself from AIDS. A Western woman attempts to blow up a condom; a samurai examines the quality of the rubber to make sure that the texture is correct, 'There are no holes in the test of this condom—you have to blow it up still farther. We don't want to be sorry and regret something later. This world is very confused these days.' 'Oh, oh, I cannot blow this up much more or it is going to pop.' " The red cartouche to the far right indicates that the setting is the "Masami-za," or Masami theater. Other cartouches identify his signatures, "Masami" and "Teraoka," and pinpoint the painting's site as Santa Monica Beach. An inscription dates the work to 1987.

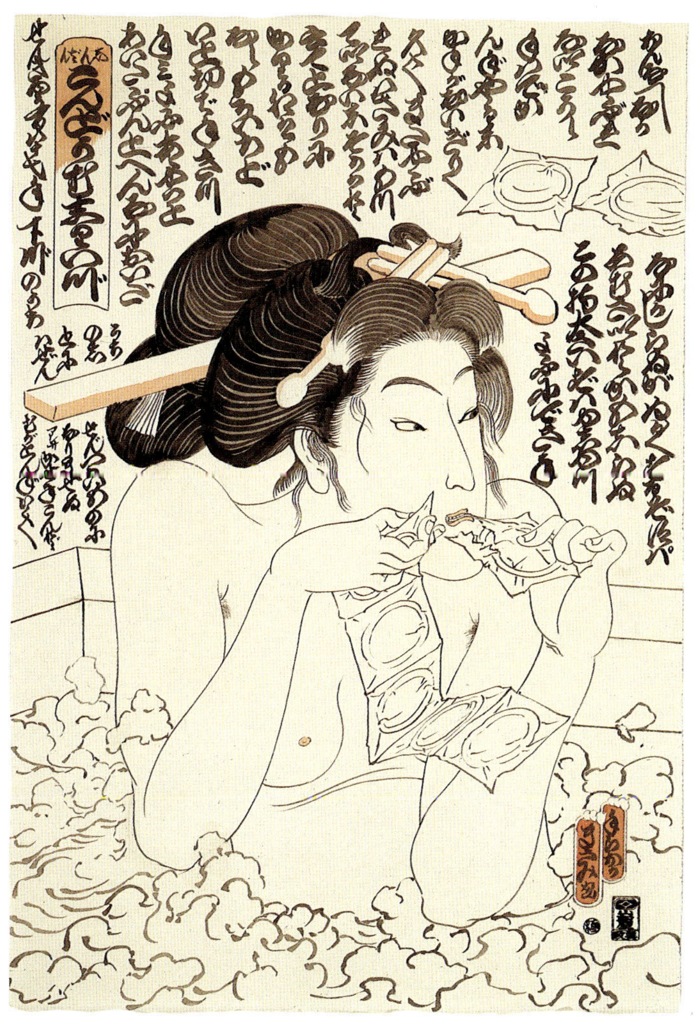

24

AIDS SERIES

GEISHA IN BATH

1987, watercolor study on paper, 22 1/4 × 15 in.
Collection of the artist

This painting was a preparatory study for *Geisha in Bath* (cat. no. 25). A geisha is seated in a wooden bathtub (*ofuro*), her hair neatly coiffured with extra-thick hairpins. Packages of condoms fly through the air as she bites open the first of a long string of condoms in preparation for the night's activities.

The *tanzaku* cartouche in the upper left corner translates "New Woodblock Condom Series," and the long inscription vividly explains the scene: "A courtesan is attempting to tear open a condom package and announces, 'Maybe I should use my teeth to tear it open.' As she tries, her teeth gnash together making the sound, '*giri giri giri*,' but alas she cannot tear open the package. Impatiently she announces, 'Well, I don't have any scissors here in the bathtub ... maybe I should go next door to borrow a pair of scissors, but then that's so inconvenient. I'm already in my bath! Maybe the *ito kiri ba* [lit. thread-cutting tooth, e.g., eye tooth] will do it this time.' Finally she succeeds, but the rubber smells so foul: 'Oh! What is this? It's so slimy!' [She has discovered the lubricant.] 'This must be spermicide. Oh no! *Kono tokudai* ... This is the giant size; this is the export model ... Damn it! My lover won't be able to use it.' A sudden breeze sends condom packages flying through the air."

25

AIDS SERIES
GEISHA IN BATH

1988, watercolor on canvas, 108 × 81 in.
Space Gallery, Los Angeles

As in the watercolor study of the same title (cat. no. 24), a courtesan (identified by Teraoka as a geisha, his symbol for traditional Japan) is seated in a wooden bathtub (*ofuro*), her coiffure, held by extra-thick hairpins, suggesting a high-ranking lady of the demimonde. Two condoms fly through the air, while she attempts to bite open a condom package in preparation for the night's social appointments. Unlike the study, the cartouche identifying the series has been omitted, and the background text surrounding the figure has been reduced and simplified. Interspersed throughout are phonetic signs in red which suggest that the text is part of a kabuki narrative chant (*jōruri*), in this case, a specific style known as *gidaiyū-bushi.* Read from right to left, the text translates: " '*Ma nakanaka akanai* ... I cannot open this at all ... I don't have scissors ... I hate to go and borrow scissors from next door ...' Finally she opens it with her teeth to be greeted with a peculiarly strong odor. She again speaks, 'This could be spermicide; it's also slimy ... Oh no, this is an export model; my boyfriend won't be able to use it!' A sudden breeze sends condom packages flying through the air. *Kon domu* [condom] *ga tonde* [fly] *yuku, yuku* [go]." Especially in erotic literature, a narrative sentence will often end with a sexual climax in which the lovers cry "*iku, iku* [go]." Teraoka cleverly parodies such narratives here.

Compared with the earlier study, this courtesan portrait possesses a monumental simplicity. There is a delicacy in the shadings and greater attention given to the rendering of the hair. Bold form and delicate, finely executed detail are blended in a composition of great elegance.

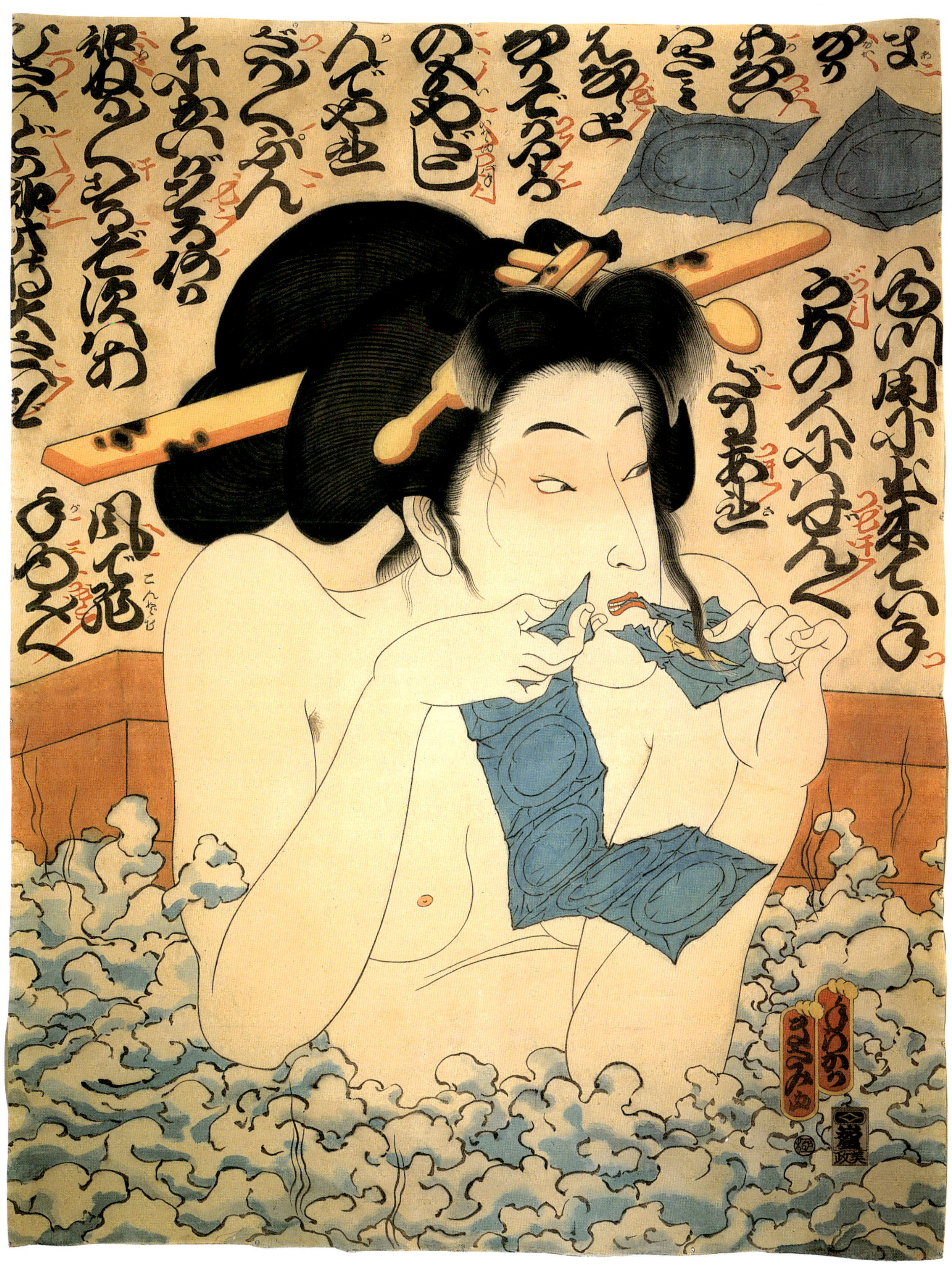

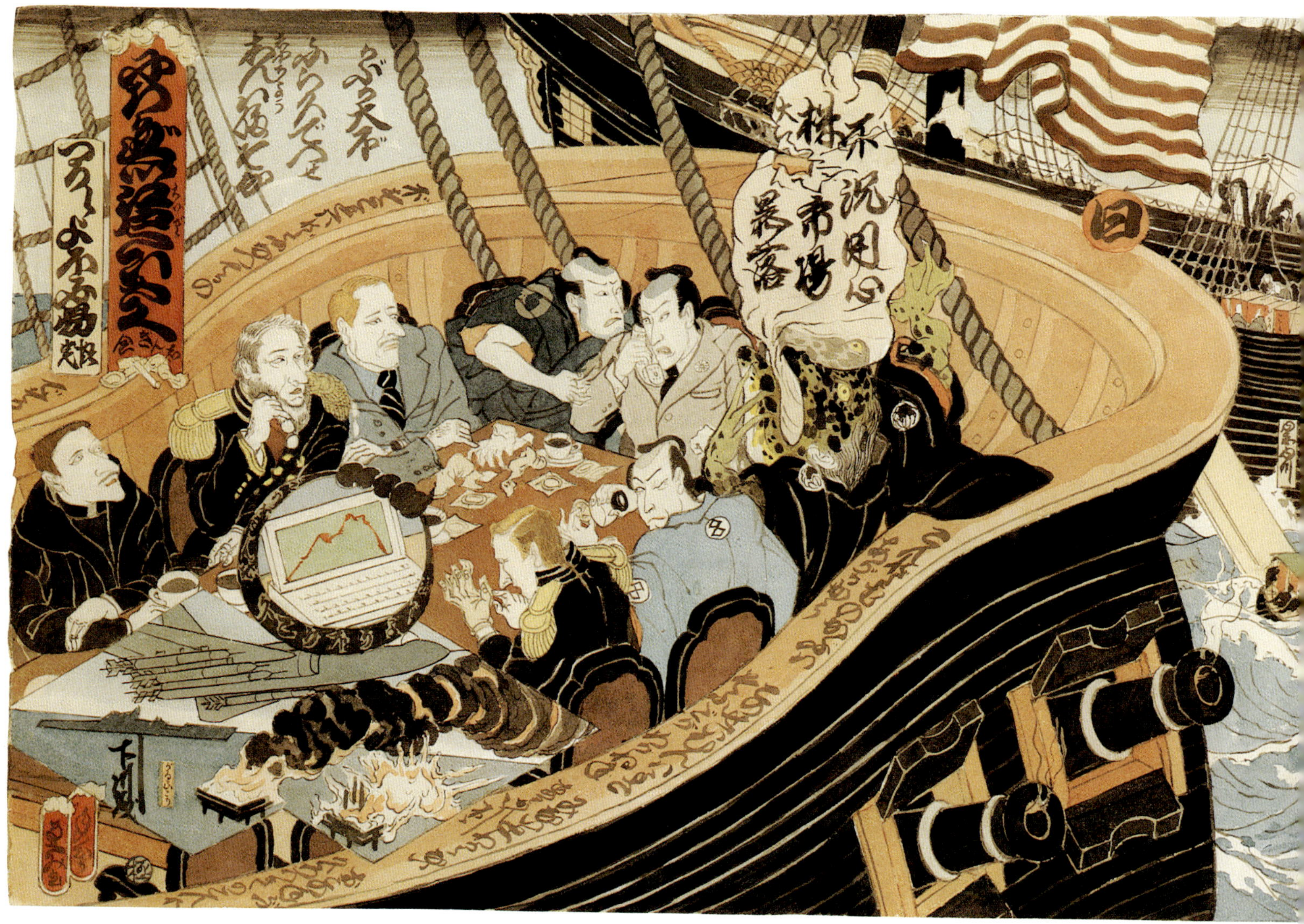

26

AIDS SERIES

CONDOM TRADE WARS

1987, watercolor study on paper, 15 × 44 in.
Space Gallery, Los Angeles

East meets West in this rendition of a predictable trade war between Japan and America. On the left is the black ship of Commodore Matthew Perry, who is returning to Japan to negotiate the delicate matter of trade balance in condom exports. In the black ship, along with Commodore Perry, are several Japanese business representatives, who are meeting with American dignitaries for commerce on the sale of American condoms in Japan. Inspecting the condoms is a business man with a toad face and body, who has just become aware of the stock market crash of October 1987; a keyboard and a screen showing the stock crash in progress appear in a floating cartouche. An inscription above translates: "Stock market crash; depression is coming." Text along the rim of the black ship and elsewhere translates: "Condom stock will go up; condom quality must be scrutinized; without a magnifying glass I cannot examine, but it looks good to the naked eye; the stock market crashed, but don't worry."

Facing the black ship is a pleasure boat carrying courtesans of all types painted in the style of the mid-nineteenth century. They are testing the American condoms for strength and endurance. "Right now we have to export quickly," a lady with a round fan announces. An old man in charge of shipping replies: "OK. It's as good as done." A lantern to the far right reads: "For export—condoms." Beyond, one can see a small American

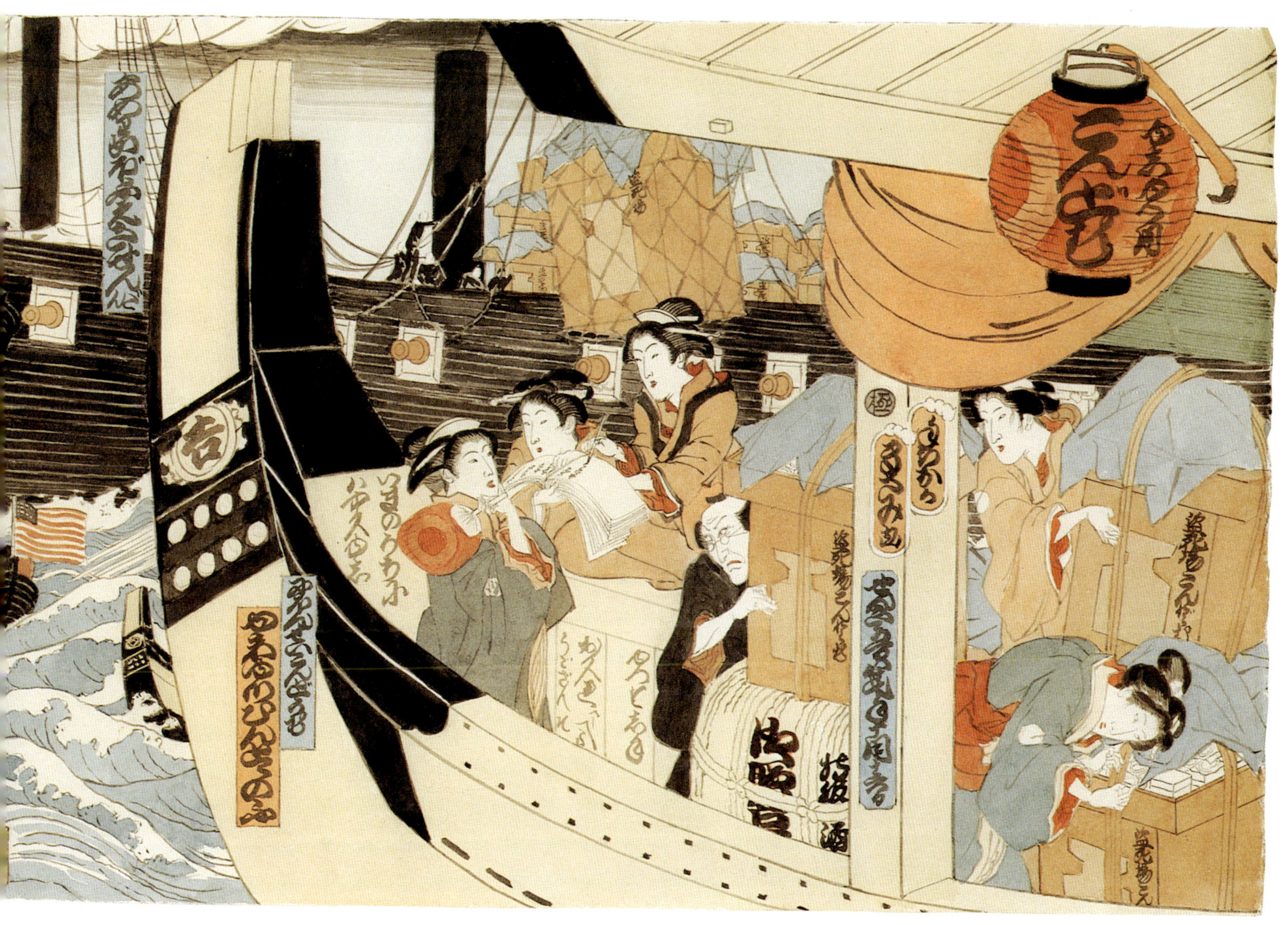

boat making its way to shore with U.S. merchandise. In still another boat farther in the distance (identified with the characters "Tō Shi Ba"), another company is engaged in the "secret" export of condoms. This is an obvious reference to the electronics company Toshiba (spelled with different characters), which dealt in a different kind of secret export to the Russians.

27

AIDS SERIES BLACK SHIPS AND GEISHA

1987, watercolor study on paper, 30 × 57 in.
Space Gallery, Los Angeles

This study, recalling a theatrical *kyōgen* (scene or interlude), offers a plethora of interesting narrative. At the entrance to her bedroom, a courtesan opens a condom with the help of the floating head of a male ghost. Emanating from the skeletal remains of his AIDS-ridden body, depicted at the far left of the composition, the ghost's head has drifted across the composition, leaving a translucent stream of phantasmal material behind him. Two courtesans sit by a warmer (*hibachi*); one stretchs a condom to test its strength. The condom is of enormous size, in keeping with the exaggeration found in erotic prints (*shunga*). Farther to the left, a seated tattooed figure also checks a large oversize condom.

All is overseen by the madam of the house, who, because this is a kabuki scene, is a kabuki *onnagata*, or female impersonator, identifiable by the orange cloth covering her head. Many of the kabuki actors of the seventeenth century, particularly the female impersonators, were men of bisexual conduct. These males proved a great source of attraction to other men, so much so that in 1652 the shogunate suppressed the theater and forced the actors to shave off their forelocks to lessen their feminine charms. To disguise this problem they took to wearing a cloth across the upper part of their foreheads. This special distinction proved to make the *onnagata* even more attractive. In this case, the *onnagata* holds a long teaching scroll, on which is written: "New educational material for sex—your spirit must be prepared for the use of condoms." In addition, two large condom packages are inscribed: "Giant size, bargain price." The brand name is "Safe "

Commodore Perry's black ship is anchored in the harbor, and in the distance are two dinosaurs and a Soviet submarine. The dinosaurs are sinking boat labeled "Tō Shi Ba" (but spelled with different characters than the electronics firm). Three insets add meaning to the scene. Two of the insets show an American trade negotiator and Japanese Prime Minister Noboru Takeshita engaged in resolving various trade frictions. Another shows Surgeon General C. Everett Koop as the "Condom Master," that is, the teacher who will train all in the proper use of the condom. A cartouche shows a smoking gun of the black ship, a reference to recent approaches to diplomatic solutions taken by the United States.

At the top of the painting, as if the entire scene were a kabuki illustration, an extensive narrative describes four different aspects of the action. To suggest that this is a kabuki narrative chant (*jōruri*), Teraoka includes two women samisen players, who help to decorate the narrative itself. The cast of the scene is given first, in heavy black writing to the far right. The scene is identified as "migi kyōgen," or "*kyōgen* of the right," but actually refers to a scene that occurs on the left.

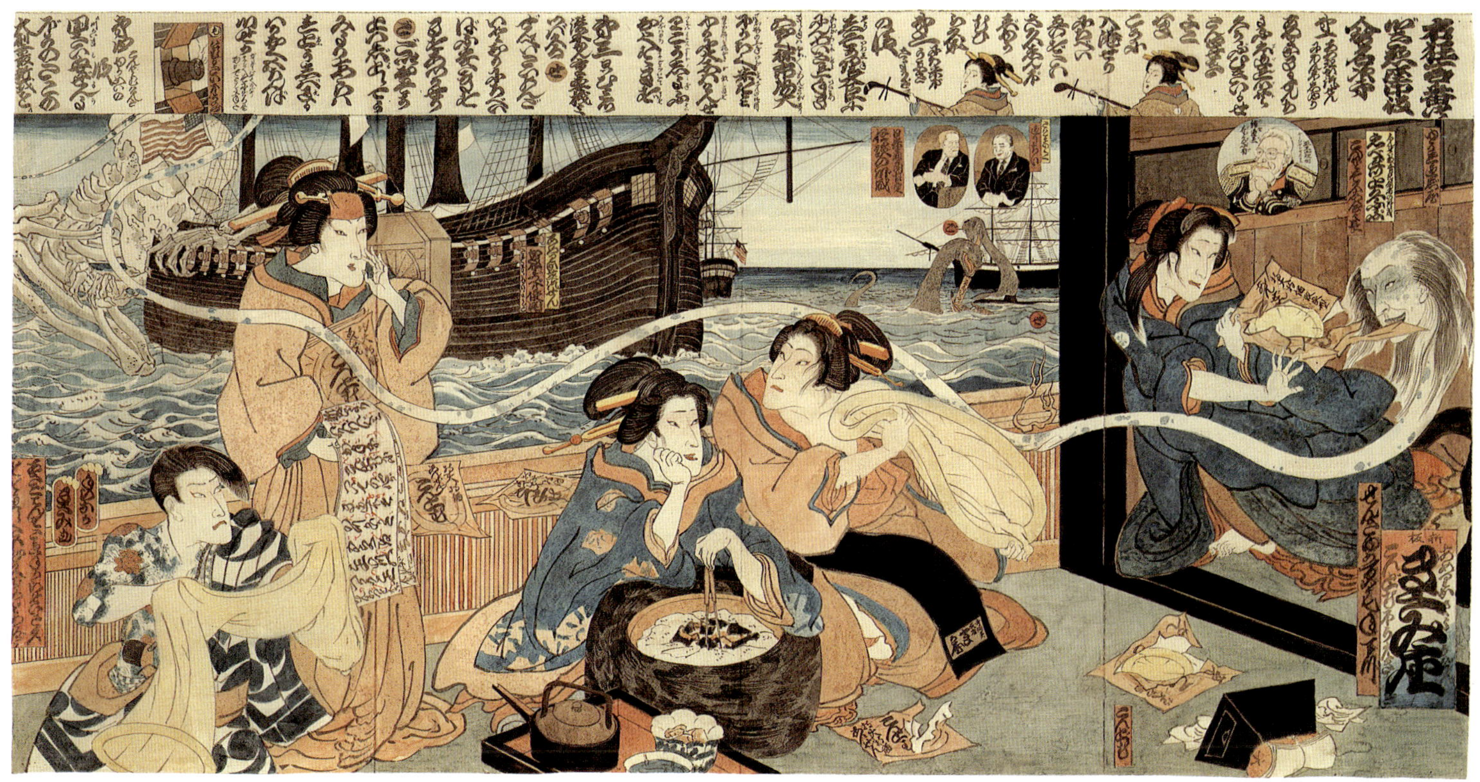

In the first scene the American black ship arrives in Japan. Surgeon General Koop is the captain of the boat and is in charge of four black ships in Tokyo Bay, anchored there for a special symposium between Japan and America.

The second sequence deals with a "Nichibei Trading Agreement" on the sale of condoms, *nichi* referring to Japan and *bei* referring to America. Negotiations are not going well and trade friction is great. The American stock market crash is also discussed.

The third scene considers the exposure of a Japanese company that sold secret information to the Russians. The narrative tells of the sinking of the "Tō Shi Ba Maru" by dinosaurs. The sound of the sinking boat, "*ga ga basa basa, jabun, jabun*," can be heard.

The final act deals with an international conference on condoms, and the training of ladies in the use of condoms, at which a super-giant improved condom is introduced from America. Teraoka cleverly uses the word *kaidan* for "meeting": it also carries the meaning of "ghost story."

The kabuki theater is identified in a large cartouche in the right corner as "Masami-za," and in a long vertical red cartouche the date of the painting, 1987, is given. Two small red cartouches on the far left, done in the style of Kunisada, identify the artist. To the left of his signature is a humorous aside, housed in a vertical cartouche, indicating that Teraoka the artist needs to have breakfast before he begins work, otherwise his eyes and energy will give out.

2 8

AIDS SERIES
MAKIKI HEIGHTS
DISASTER

1987, watercolor study on paper, 30 × 60 in.
Space Gallery, Los Angeles

This splendid painting is rich in iconography and meaning. To the lower right is a seated man holding a long scroll. He is identified by Teraoka as the "Condom Master," and in his hands he holds an instruction scroll on the proper use of condoms so that one can avoid catching the AIDS virus. On the ground next to him are the wrappers of two condoms, one of which has been opened, and a magnifying glass used to check their quality. A large, grotesque snake, exhausted, its tongue hanging out, has been captured in a huge condom by a mountain priest (*yamabushi*) and a Caucasian woman (Lynda Hess). Aiding this bizarre duo is a balding Caucasian with angular features dressed in a traditional kimono. Clearly the snake is the symbol of the male sexual organ infected with the AIDS virus. Blood-sucking bats are included in the design as ill omens and perhaps even as carriers of the disease. The effect is particularly startling, since the artist has depicted the figures and snake in a sustained pose known in kabuki as a *mie*. The head of another much larger snake intrudes into the scene, suggesting that a more toxic virus or plague might await man in the future.

In the middle of the composition a warrior is tied to a tomb sign. He is held not by rope but by a snake, suggesting that the samurai is doomed to die of the deadly plague. Next to him are the skeletal remains of his girlfriend. In the foreground, to the left, a toad, a symbol for the next more deadly generation of AIDS, devours a snake, which has attacked two lovers resting on a veranda and is in the process of eating his female victim.

Completing the image are two ghost heads floating through the air and looking on in horror. As a backdrop Teraoka has used the exotic trees of Makiki Heights, their phallic seedpods hanging down as if they were dangling from a meat rack. At the base of the scene is the suggestion of a flood, a topical reference to the great flood that occurred on New Year's Eve of 1987 on Oahu. The entire fantasy is reminiscent of kabuki illustrated books (*eiri-kyōgen bon*), and the floating heads recall the feudal Japanese *kubijikken* syndrome of chopping off the head of an enemy to resolve social and political problems.

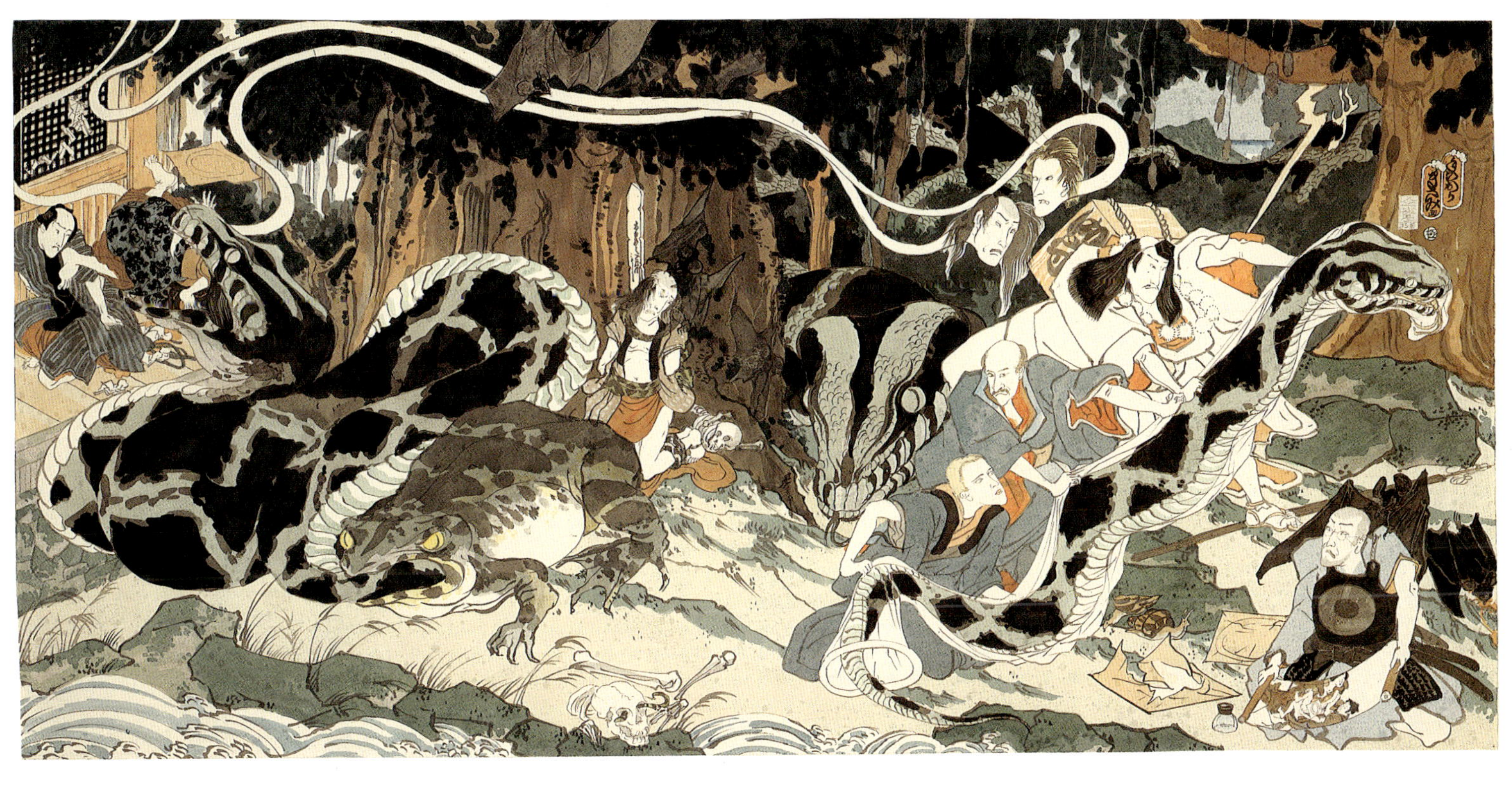

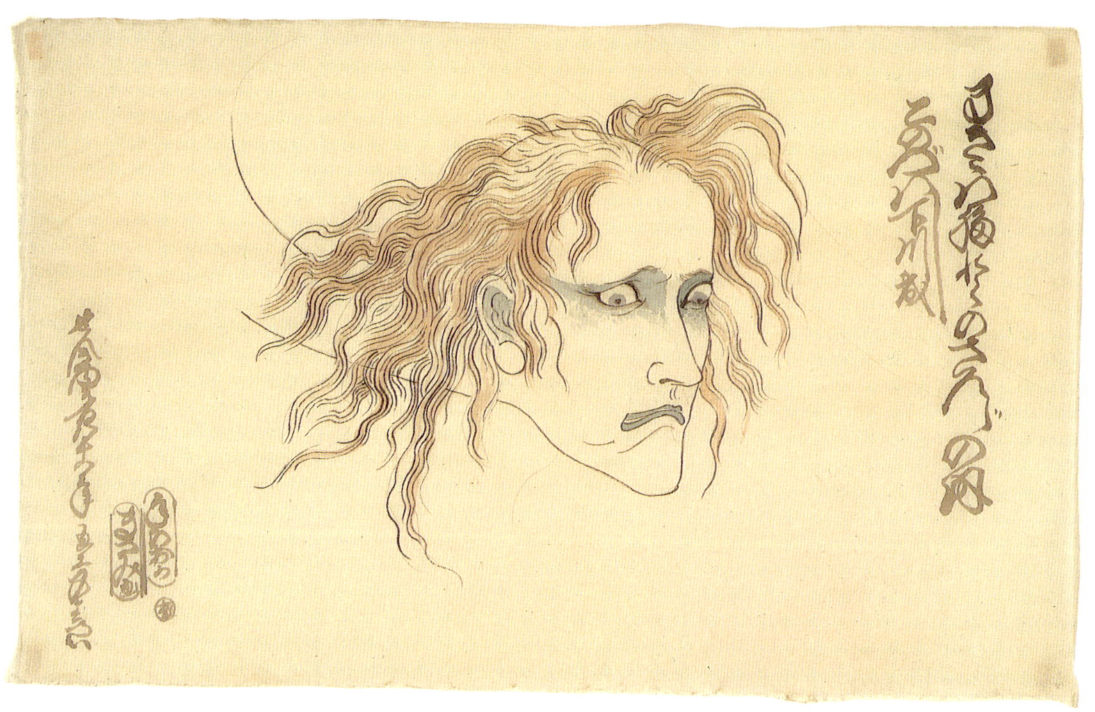

29

AIDS SERIES MAKIKI HEIGHTS DISASTER: GHOST WOMAN

1988, watercolor study on paper, 12 × 19 in.
Space Gallery, Los Angeles

The rendering of this disembodied head of a ghost woman was no doubt inspired by the imagery of the ghost of Oiwa as depicted in the kabuki play *Yotsuya Kaidan*. Oiwa, whose name appears in connection with *American Kabuki/Oishiiwa* (cat. no. 18), was cruelly murdered by her husband but came back from her grave to wreak bloody vengeance. Here her dismembered visage has metamorphosed into a hypnotic glare. The connection between Oiwa's circumstance and that of an AIDS victim is clearly implied: Oiwa was poisoned by her philandering husband, as such husbands in today's society might very well pass on the deadly AIDS virus to their partners. The sketch is reminiscent of a famous verse written in the late spring of 1849 by Katsushika Hokusai, who died at the age of eighty-nine. His parting haiku reads, "Even as a ghost I'll tread the summer moors."

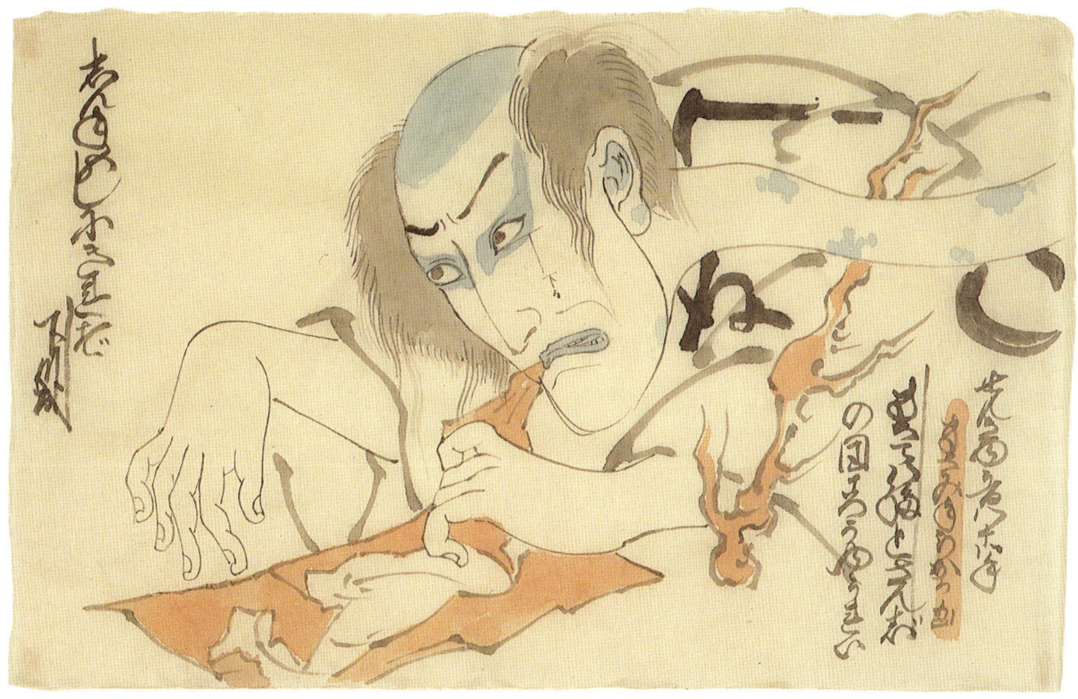

30

AIDS SERIES MAKIKI HEIGHTS DISASTER: DANJŪRŌ

1988, watercolor study on paper, 12 × 19 in.
Space Gallery, Los Angeles

This brush painting, a watercolor sketch for a larger painting, depicts Ichikawa Danjūrō VII (1791–1858). The compiler of the best plays in the repertoire of the Ichikawa family, Danjūrō VII was regarded as one of the most accomplished and handsome kabuki actors in the famous lineage. Idolized by the ladies of Edo (old Tokyo), this star was particularly famous for his portrayal of Gōrō in the Soga drama entitled *Kongen Kusazuri-biki*. For his kimono he invented a special rebus design composed of a sickle (*kama*), a circle (*wa*), and the hiragana syllable *nu*, which together make up the word *kamawanu*, or "I don't care." This rebus might have inspired Teraoka to portray the famed actor as the prototype for a high-risk playboy. So handsome a personage was Danjūrō VII that women would collect articles of his clothing, and it is even claimed that if the great actor would spit on the street, women would collect the sputum in their handkerchiefs and keep it as a souvenir.

Danjūrō VII perfected the use of face paint to distinguish character types in kabuki plays and is credited with bringing the *bokashi* method of shading or gradation to a new level of perfection. He introduced the fundamental procedure of making the face appear thinner or larger, and he devised *ippon-guma*, in which the eyes and eyebrows are given a red (*beni*) linear accent to add a youthful appearance to the face. This makeup was particularly favored for roles requiring a handsome appearance and was quite distinct from the makeup used for nonhuman types, including gods and ghosts, in which red was replaced by blue indigo.

Teraoka depicted Danjūrō VII attempting, with little success, to open a condom package. The blue makeup suggests he is already dead but that his soul still lives on. This position as a "living-dead" person is reflected in the inscription to the left, which can be translated, "He died, but his soul hasn't really passed on yet; it wanders around." Nowhere in Teraoka's work does one find a more poignant expression of the dilemma faced by AIDS victims.

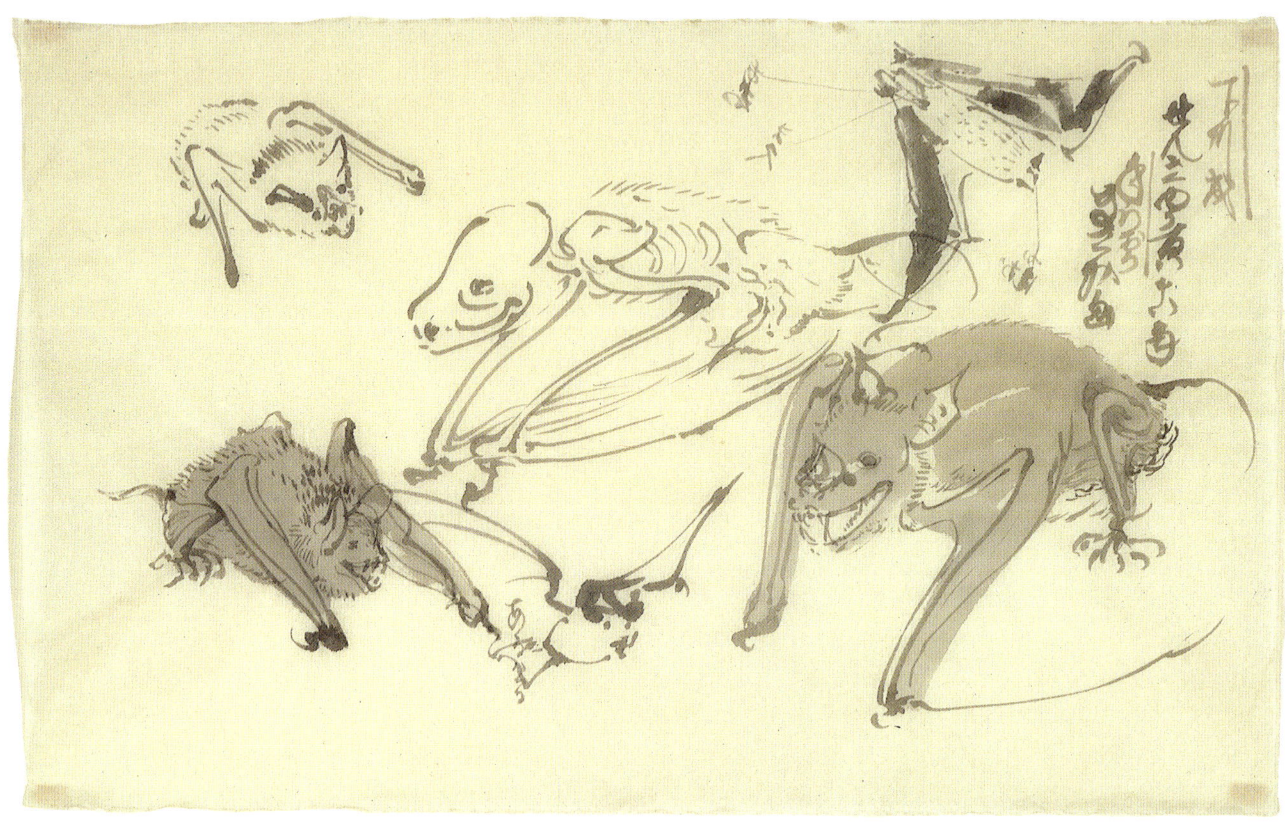

31

AIDS SERIES MAKIKI HEIGHTS DISASTER: VAMPIRE BATS

1988, watercolor study on paper, 12 × 19 in.
Space Gallery, Los Angeles

The fluid watercolor line in the animated rendering of vampire bats in this black and white sketch says much about Teraoka's method. The sketches are reminiscent of Hokusai's famous *manga*, figural and animal studies that seem to come to life and spill over the page. The inscription reads "Masami" and dates the work to 1988. Another inscription was painted on the back side of the thin mulberry paper and shows through in reverse.

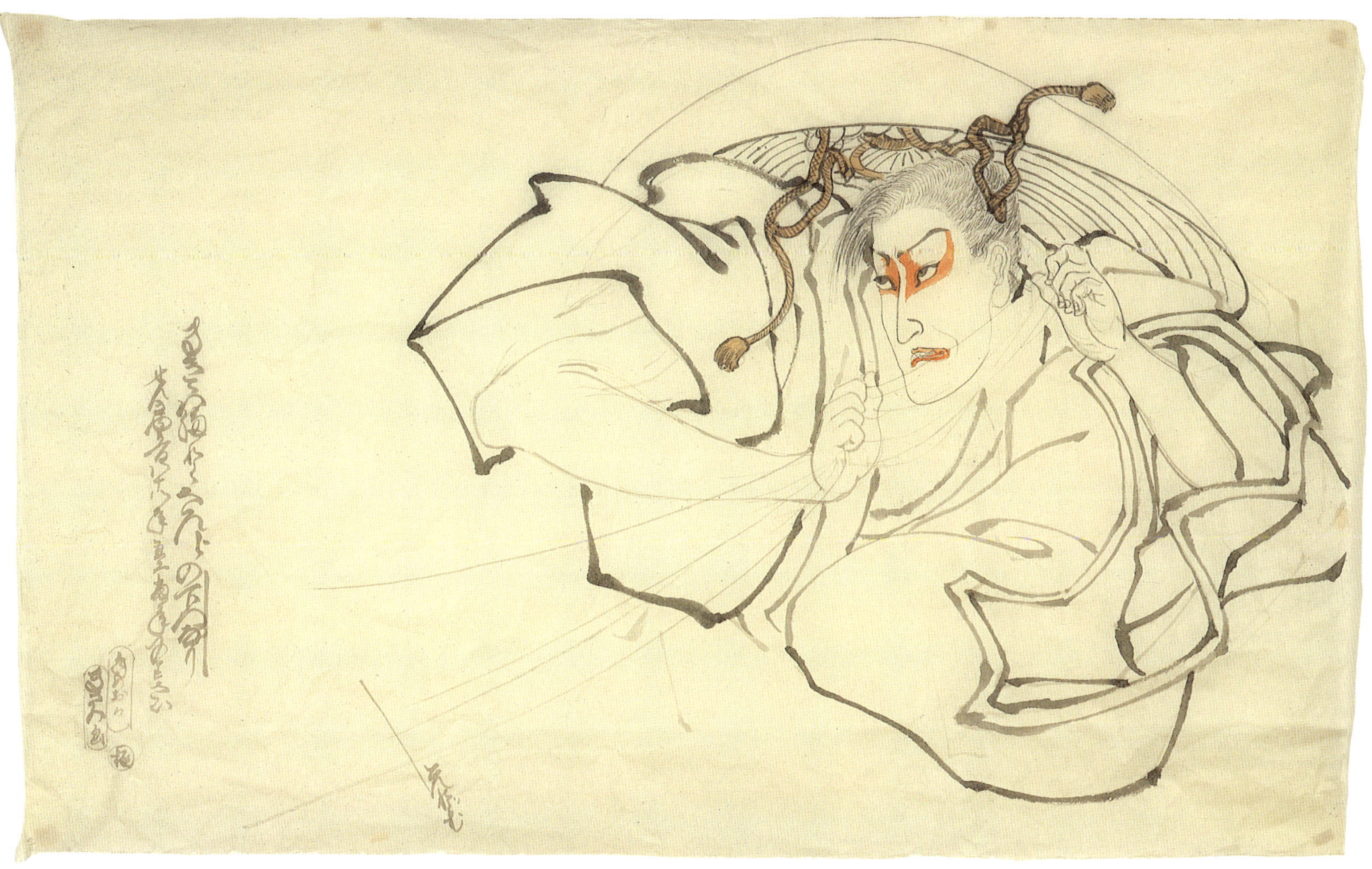

32

AIDS SERIES

MAKIKI HEIGHTS

DISASTER:

SAMURAI

1988, watercolor study on paper, 24 1/2 × 38 1/2 in.

Space Gallery, Los Angeles

This particular study for the figure of a samurai in *Makiki Heights Disaster* (cat. no. 33) comes close to the finished version. The samurai wears a big basket hat (*kasa*), umbrella-shaped and made of reed, used to guard against the elements and at times to conceal the wearer's identity. The style shown here, a traveling hat (*dōchū gasa*), was often worn by personages of the samurai class, but sometimes by commoners when traveling. In the larger painting, the samurai uses the hat to protect himself from the venom of a large snake, the symbol for AIDS in Teraoka's kabuki-inspired iconography. Also present in this composition is a large condom, which will be used to try to capture the poisonous snake and prevent it from spreading its venom.

33

AIDS SERIES
MAKIKI HEIGHTS DISASTER

1988, watercolor on paper, mounted as a four-panel screen, 77 1/2 × 155 in.
Space Gallery, Los Angeles

The latest realization of *Makiki Heights Disaster* is this tour-de-force four-panel screen, done in watercolor using the broad calligraphic line of the traditional Japanese brush (*fude*). The painting is identified to the far right in cartouche as "Snake and Toad." The narrative reads from right to left in the traditional manner of a handscroll and opens with a scene of two lovers resting on the veranda of a temple structure. The man is grimacing, for the woman has just announced that they will have to use a condom. Around them are rumpled tissues, a traditional symbol for sexual activity. The woman holds a huge condom package, on which is written, "giant-size model, newly improved, special sale (30% discount)." Her male counterpart holds an illustrated book entitled "On the Use of Condoms," which reads in part: "Try not to be bitten by poisonous snakes; you must use a condom . . ." Behind the amorous partners is a lattice window, on which a number of shinto fortune-telling papers (*omikuji*) have been tied, suggesting perhaps the ominousness of predicting the future.

The scene is placed in Makiki Heights, and in the distance, a glimpse of Diamond Head can be seen. Both Makiki Heights and Diamond Head are identified in cartouche to the left. The lushness of the Hawaiian setting is given a Gothic heaviness. Vampire bats hover throughout the scene; lightning streaks signify the awesome power of nature. Weaving in and out of the composition are the luminous trails of two disembodied ghost heads.

The main focus of the right half of the screen is a huge coiled snake, symbol of the AIDS virus and its means of transmission, being eaten by a giant grotesque toad. This theme, identified in cartouche as the title of the screen, offers one of the main messages of the work. Traditionally, the toad is a fearsome animal who, within the ukiyo-e world, is always depicted as a bad ghost. Teraoka's iconography suggests that an even fiercer virus than AIDS awaits us—the ecological nightmares caused by man have come full circle, and nature now revolts against man himself.

The second focus of the complex composition, in the left half of the screen, features a samurai and a Caucasian woman, identified in cartouche as Lynda Hess, attempting to open a huge condom package. A monstrous snake is shedding a torn condom and spitting sperm-like venom at the samurai. To protect himself, the warrior has covered his head with his umbrella-like *kasa* hat (see cat. no. 32 for a study of this detail). Overseeing this bizarre scene is U.S. Surgeon General C. Everett Koop, carefully delineated so that his face is recognizable. He is dressed in white robes decorated with calligraphy, an attire reminiscent of garments worn by a *yamabushi*, or mountain priest, but also associated with death (white robes are used in ritual suicide, *seppuku*). The characters on the white field of the robe translate "Condom Master." The waters below represent a flood that struck Oahu on New Year's Eve of 1987, taken by Teraoka as an ominous sign of nature's displeasure with man. Above are the heads of a Western female ghost with flowing blonde locks and of Danjūrō VII, identified in cartouche.

Details abound in this screen. For example, in the second panel from the right is a skull; a snake, also used by Teraoka as a symbol of the next generation of AIDS virus, slides through its fissures. Surgeon General Koop holds a scroll in his hand on which are painted lovely mushrooms (*matsutake*) and pine needles. The pine needles symbolize drug needles (one of the two main ways of acquiring the dread disease), and the mushrooms refer to the male sexual organ. The traditional combination of *matsutake* and pine needles is given new and explicit meaning here. The text of the scroll reads: "*kondo mo kondomu shiyō* ... this time let's use a condom [Teraoka cleverly alliterates the sound of condom in two languages] ... Gynecologists are afraid because of the poor health of the American cervix, according to Surgeon General Koop."

The painting represents a synthesis of ideas accumulated over a year and took many months to complete. The results say much of Teraoka's method and of his commitment to communicating the perils of today's world.

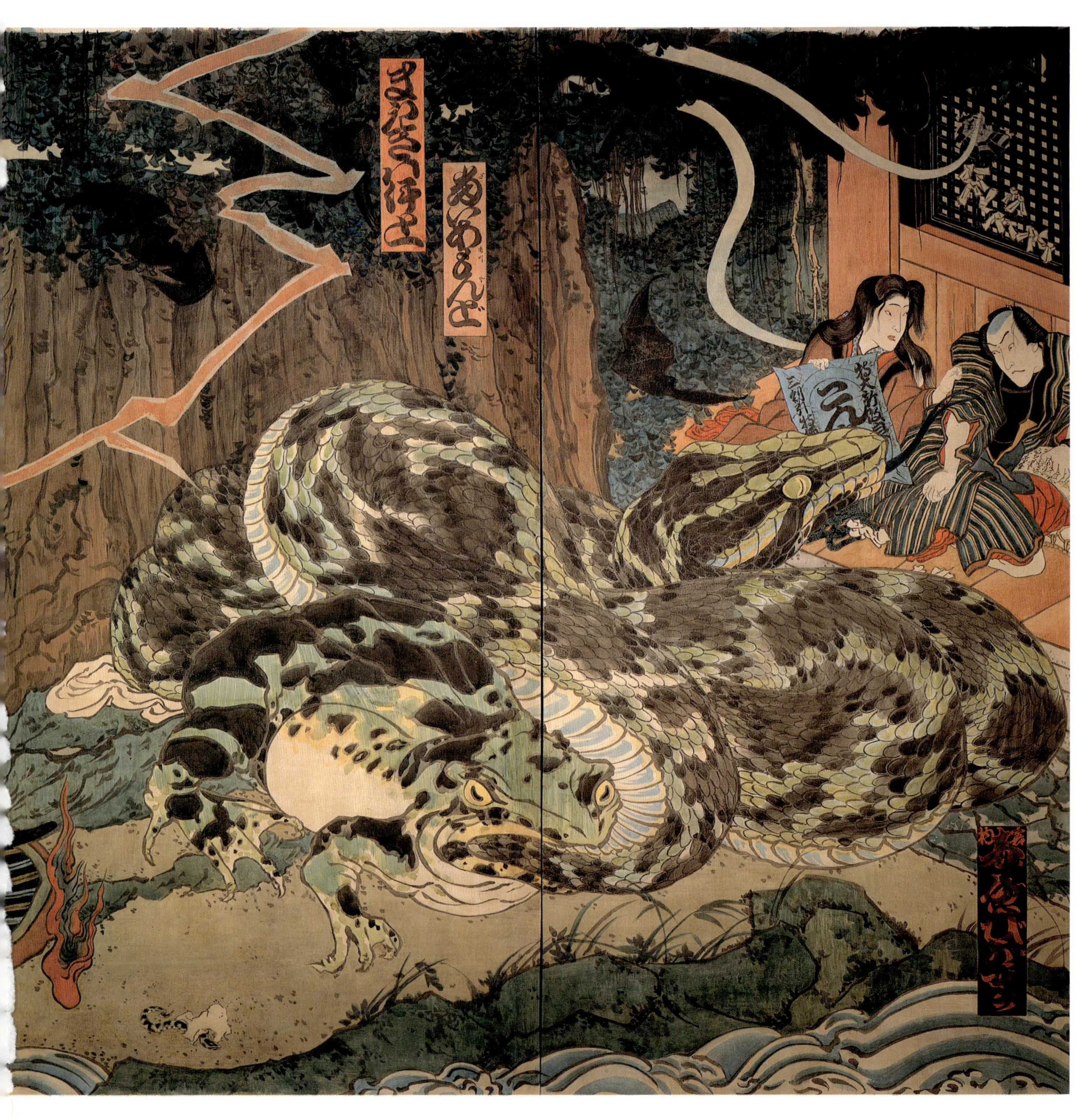

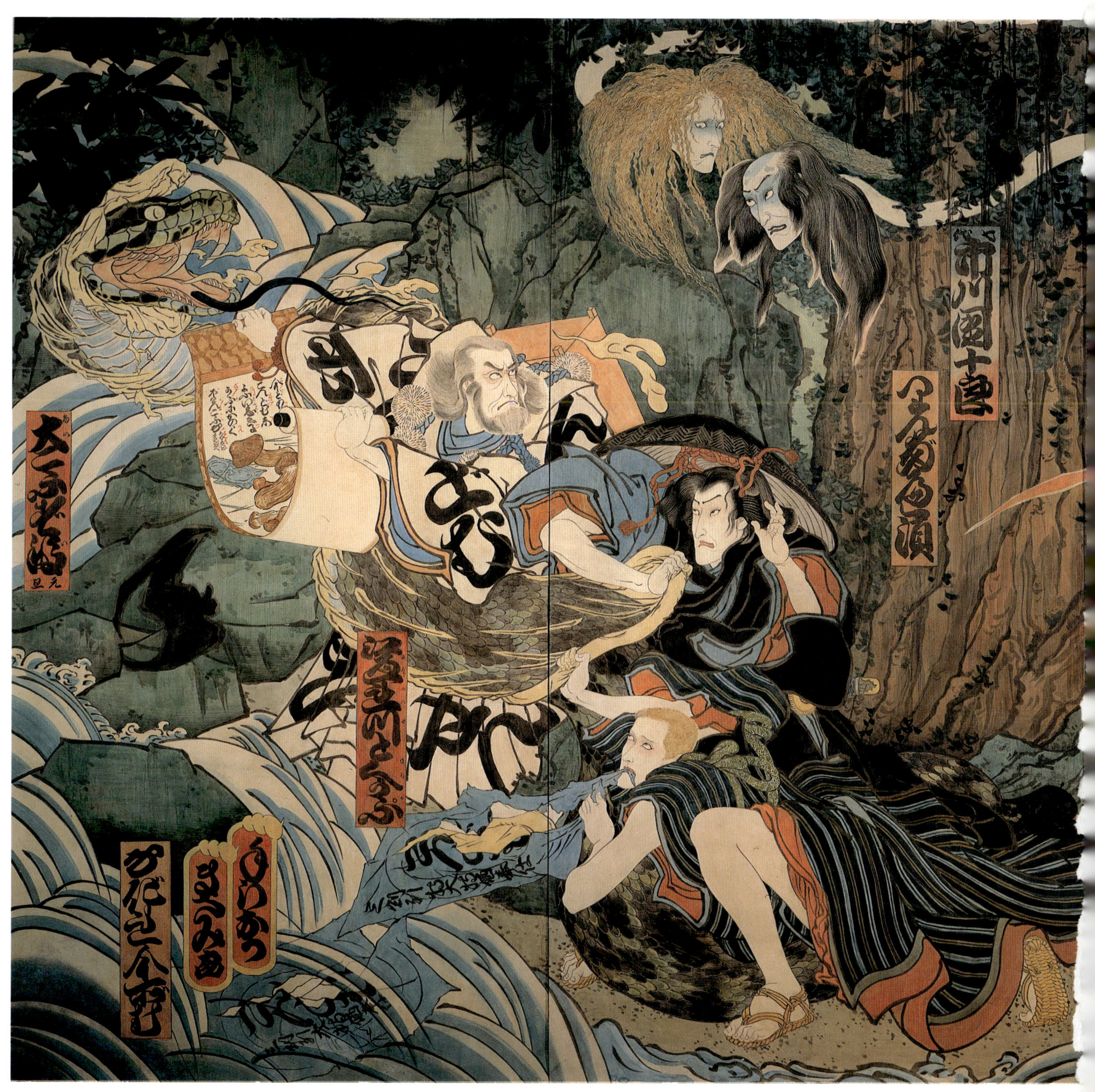
市川團十郎

BIOGRAPHY

Born in 1936 in Onomichi, Japan

EDUCATION

1968 Otis Art Institute, Los Angeles, B.A., M.F.A.

1959 Kwansei Gakuin University, Kobe, Japan, B.A.

GRANTS AND AWARDS

1980–81 National Endowment for the Arts, Artists Fellowship

1978 Kay Nielsen Memorial Purchase Award through the Graphic Arts Council, Los Angeles County Museum of Art

SELECTED SOLO EXHIBITIONS

1988 Space Gallery, Los Angeles (also 1986, 1985, 1979, 1977, 1975)

1986 Monterey Peninsula Museum of Art, California

1985 Allport Associates Gallery, San Francisco

Amerika Haus, United States Cultural Center, Berlin

Santa Barbara Contemporary Arts Forum, California, *Teraoka Erotica*

1983 Jacksonville Art Museum, Florida

Japanese-American Community and Cultural Center, Los Angeles

The Oakland Museum, California

Santa Ana College, California

1981 Zolla/Lieberman Gallery, Chicago, *Masami Teraoka/The Takeover of East and West*

1980 Jehu Gallery, San Francisco, *Prints by Masami Teraoka*

1979 Whitney Museum of American Art, New York (traveling exhibition)

1977 Santa Barbara Museum of Art, California

1976 The Minneapolis Institute of Arts, *La Brea Tar Pits Suite*

1973 David Stuart Gallery, Los Angeles

International Museum of Erotic Art, San Francisco

SELECTED GROUP EXHIBITIONS

1987 Los Angeles County Museum of Art, *Avant-Garde in The Eighties*

San Francisco Museum of Modern Art

Taipei Fine Arts Museum, Taiwan, *Contemporary Southern Californian Art*

Worcester Art Museum, Massachusetts, *Surimono Mokuhanga*

1986 The Balch Institute for Ethnic Studies, Philadelphia, *The American Experience: Contemporary Immigrant Artists*

Galleries of the Claremont Colleges, California, *East/West: Contemporary Asian-American Art in Los Angeles*

IBM Gallery of Science and Art, *New York*

Newspace, Los Angeles, *Dark Natures*

Sydney, Australia, *The Biennale of Sydney*

Visual Arts Center of Alaska, Anchorage, *Symbols and Narratives*

Walker Art Center, Minneapolis, *Tokyo: Form and Spirit* (traveling exhibition)

Willard Gallery, New York

1984 C. N. Gorman Museum, University of California, Davis, *Masami Teraoka/ Ben Sakoguchi*

Clark Arts Center Gallery, Rockford College, Rockford, Illinois, *National Watercolor Invitational*

Modernism, San Francisco, *Drawings by 50 California Artists*

Museo Rufino Tamayo, Mexico City, *El Arte Narrativo/Pintura Narrativo Mexicana* (traveling exhibition)

1983 American Academy and Institute of Arts and Letters, New York, *Hassam and Speicher Fund Purchase Exhibition*

Corcoran Gallery of Art, Washington, D.C., *38th Corcoran Biennial of American Painting/Second Western States Exhibition* (traveling exhibition)

1981 Art Center College of Design, Pasadena, California, *Decade: Los Angeles Painting in the Seventies*

Laguna Beach Museum of Art, California, *Works on Paper from Newport Harbor Art Museum*

Los Angeles Institute of Contemporary Art, *Humor in Art*

Montgomery and Lang Galleries, Claremont College, Claremont, California, *Professor's Choice*

Western Association of Art Museums, *Deja Vu: Masterpieces Updated* (traveling exhibition)

1980 Albuquerque Museum, New Mexico, *Katachi: Form and Spirit in Japanese Art*

1979 Corcoran Gallery of Art, Washington, D.C., *Selections from the Frederick Weisman Company Collection of California Art*

Los Angeles Municipal Art Gallery, *The Artist as Social Critic*

1978 The Art Museum and Galleries, California State University, Long Beach, *The Frederick Weisman Company Collection of California Art*

Space Gallery, Los Angeles, *Thanatopsis/Contemplations on Death*

Whitney Museum of American Art, New York, *Art About Art* (traveling exhibition)

1977 California State University, Los Angeles, *Miniature*

1976 California State University, San Bernardino, *Self-Portrait, Self-Reference*

Los Angeles County Museum of Art, *L.A. 8*

Museum of Modern Art, New York, *New Work/California*

1975 Los Angeles Institute of Contemporary Art, *Current Concerns—Part II*

Los Angeles Municipal Art Gallery, *Impetus—The Creative Process*

Newport Harbor Art Museum, Newport Beach, California, *New Acquisitions, Extended Loans, and Selected Works*

Newport Harbor Art Museum, Newport Beach, California, *4x8 + 4x4*

1974 Baxter Art Gallery, California Institute of Technology, Pasadena, *In the Japanese Tradition*

COMMISSIONS

1984 Cover for *The Arts-Extension Catalogue,* University of California, Los Angeles, *New Views of Mt. Fuji/Whale and Samurai*

1984 Cover for *Extension Catalogue,* University of California, Los Angeles, *McDonald's Hamburgers Invading Japan/Chochin-me*

1981 Cover for *Time* magazine, March 30, 1981, *Zangyo Samurai*

SELECTED COLLECTIONS

Achenbach Foundation for the Graphic Arts, Fine Arts Museums of San Francisco
Albuquerque Museum, New Mexico
Atlantic Richfield Company, Los Angeles
California State University, Los Angeles
Cedars-Sinai Medical Center, Los Angeles
Continental Insurance Company, New York
Cray Research Inc. and Walker Art Center, Minneapolis
The Federal Reserve Bank of San Francisco
Jacksonville Art Museum, Florida
Laguna Beach Museum of Art, California
Los Angeles County Museum of Art
Mid-Atlantic Toyota Corporation, Glen Burnie, Maryland
The Minneapolis Institute of Arts
National Museum of American Art, Washington, D.C.
National Portrait Gallery, Washington, D.C.
Newport Harbor Art Museum, Newport Beach, California
The Oakland Museum, California
Santa Barbara Art Museum, California
Sears Roebuck Company, Chicago
Frederick R. Weisman Collection, Los Angeles
Worcester Art Museum, Massachusetts

BIBLIOGRAPHY

CATALOGUES AND BOOKS

Addiss, Stephen, and Pat Fister. *Katachi: Form and Spirit in Japanese Art.* Albuquerque, N. Mex.: Albuquerque Museum, 1980.

Alcuaz, Maria de. *Contemporary Southern Californian Art.* Taipei: Fine Arts Museum, 1988.

Art Center College of Design. *Decade: Los Angeles Painting in the Seventies.* Pasadena, Calif., 1981.

Ballatore, Sandy. *Miniature.* Los Angeles: California State University, 1977.

The Biennale of Sydney. Sydney, Australia, 1986.

Cedars-Sinai Medical Center. *Exhibition '76, '77.* Los Angeles, 1978.

Fox, Howard N. *Avant-Garde in The Eighties.* Los Angeles: Los Angeles County Museum of Art, 1987.

Friedman, Mildred, ed. *Tokyo: Form and Spirit.* Minneapolis and New York: Walker Art Center and Harry N. Abrams, Inc., 1986.

Glenn, Constance. *The Frederick Weisman Company Collection of California Art.* Long Beach, Calif.: California State University, 1978.

Haggerty, Gerard. *Masami Teraoka.* Jacksonville, Fla.: Jacksonville Art Museum, 1983.

———. *Masami Teraoka.* Oakland, Calif.: The Oakland Museum, 1983.

———. *Teraoka Erotica.* Santa Barbara, Calif.: Santa Barbara Contemporary Arts Forum, 1985.

Kurtz, Bruce D. *El Arte Narrativo/Pintura Narrativo Mexicana.* Mexico City: Museo Rufino Tamayo, 1984.

Lee, Hon-Ching. *National Watercolor Invitational.* Rockford, Ill.: Rockford College, 1984.

Link, Howard A. *Masami Teraoka.* New York: Whitney Museum of American Art, 1979.

Lipman, Jean, and Richard Marshall. *Art About Art.* New York: E. P. Dutton, 1978.

MacNaughton, Mary. *East/West: Contemporary Asian-American Art in Los Angeles.* Claremont, Calif.: Galleries of the Claremont Colleges, 1986.

Marrow, Marva. *Inside the L.A. Artist.* Salt Lake City: Peregrine Smith Books, 1988.

McCabe, Cynthia Jaffee, et al. *The American Experience: Contemporary Immigrant Artists.* Philadelphia: The Balch Institute for Ethnic Studies, 1985.

Orr-Cahall, Christina, ed. *The Art of California: Selected Works from the Collection of the Oakland Museum.* San Francisco: Oakland Museum Art Department and Chronicle Books, 1984.

Steen, Ronald E. *Deja Vu: Masterpieces Updated.* Downey, Calif.: Downey Museum of Art and Citrus Community College, 1978.

Tuchman, Maurice. *L.A. 8.* Los Angeles: Los Angeles County Museum of Art, 1976.

SELECTED ARTICLES AND REVIEWS

"About the Cover Artist, Masami Teraoka." *Extension Catalogue,* University of California, Los Angeles, Winter Quarter, January 3, 1984.

Arbient, Lys Boot. "Teraoka Blends the Centuries." *The Union Daily* (Long Beach, Calif.), February 1, 1983.

Berger, Leslie. "Visions of a New West." *The Washington Post,* February 2, 1983.

Bermann-Enn, Beate. "Masami Teraoka." *Artscene,* February 1985.

Campbell, Mary. "Teraoka's Works Mold East, West." *Jacksonville Journal* (Florida), February 24, 1983.

Flanigan, James C. "Western Artists Evoke Humor, Horror of New West." *The Oregonian* (Portland), February 8, 1983.

Frank, Peter. "Glimpsing the Nature of the True West." *Newsday*, April 8, 1984.

Glueck, Grace. "Childe Hassam's Legacy Continues to Flower." *The New York Times*, November 27, 1983.

Ianco-Starrels, Josine. "Asia Meets America—A Blend of Traditions." *Los Angeles Times*, March 2, 1986.

Lifton, Sarah. "Making Waves with Culture Clash." *L.A. Reader*, February 15, 1985.

Manuel, Susan. "Artist Looks at AIDS." *The Star Bulletin* (Honolulu), November 2, 1987.

Marrow, Elizabeth Chase. *The Florida Times Union, Jacksonville Journal*, February 13, 1983.

"Masami Teraoka/Erotic Works at CAF." *Daily News* (Los Angeles), January 10, 1985.

McDonald, Robert. "Surveying Drawing in California." *Artweek*, January 21, 1984.

McKenna, Kristine. "East/West: A Collision of Cultures." *Los Angeles Times*, March 27, 1986.

Muchnic, Suzanne. "Teraoka and the Art of Culture Shock." *Los Angeles Times*, January 12, 1985.

———. "Teraoka Brings Beauty to an Ugly Theme." *Los Angeles Times*, December 26, 1986.

Museum of Contemporary Art, Los Angeles. *The Contemporary*, Summer 1986.

Nicholson, Chuck. "The Masters of Adaptation." *Artweek*, October 11, 1986.

Richard, Paul. "The Range of the West." *The Washington Post*, February 2, 1983.

Scheib, Elizabeth. "Masami Teraoka: Bi-Cultural Double-Take." *The Japan Times*, March 5, 1985.

Silverman, Robert. "East Meets West, Post Modern Style." *Art in America*, May 1987.

Tarshis, Jerome. "Mustache on the Mona Lisa." *MD Magazine*, June 1984.

Trowbridge, David. "Masami Teraoka at Pamela Auchincloss." *Images & Issues*, January/February 1984.

Woodard, Josef. "Cross Cultural Erotica." *Artweek*, February 23, 1985.

Yim, Susan. "Masami Teraoka's 20th Century Floating World." *The Star Bulletin & Advertiser* (Honolulu), February 5, 1984.

———. "AIDS as American Kabuki." *The Honolulu Advertiser,* October 15, 1987.

LENDERS TO THE EXHIBITION

Brad and Penelope Broffman, Los Angeles

Jan and Joe Cobert

Edward Den Lau, Los Angeles

Mr. and Mrs. Robert Marin, Los Angeles

Terry Rhodes, Midland, Texas

Space Gallery, Los Angeles

Masami Teraoka, Honolulu

Several private collections

THE CONTEMPORARY MUSEUM

BOARD OF TRUSTEES